1500

FRANK LLOYD WRIGHT
YEAR BY YEAR

FRANK LLOYD WRIGHT
YEAR BY YEAR

Iain Thomson

PRC

Acknowledgments

All photography was taken by Simon Clay (© Chrysalis Images), including the cover photography, with the exception of the photographs on the following pages:

Page 7 courtesy of The Metropolitan Museum of Art, Edward Pearce Casey Fund, 1982. (1982.1051.1)

Pages 8 and 9 courtesy of The Froebel Archive for Childhood Studies, University of Surrey, England

Page 10 courtesy of The Dana-Thomas House (The Illinois Historic Preservation Agency)

Page 13 courtesy of Jeffery Howe

Page 19 (Catherine Wright) © The Frank Lloyd Wright Foundation

Pages 30-31, 32, 75, 84, 160, 161, 162, 224 (bottom), 225, 271, 272, 317, 337, 339, 380, 381, 382, 383, 400, 401, 414, 415, 416-417 courtesy of Alan Weintraub/Arcaid

Page 77 © Frank Lloyd Wright Foundation, Taliesin West, Arizona (Reference 0105.001)

Page 107 (top) © Frank Lloyd Wright Foundation, Taliesin West, Arizona (Larkin Co. Administration Building – Reference 0403.0030)

Pages 144-145 courtesy of © Matt Phalen

Pages 166-167 © Frank Lloyd Wright Foundation, Taliesin West, Arizona (Taliesin I – Reference 1104.0005)

Pages 180-181 © Frank Lloyd Wright Foundation, Taliesin West, Arizona (Midway Gardens – Reference 1401.0032)

Pages 184-185 © Ezra Stoller/ESTO/Arcaid

Page 203 © Yodogawa Steel Company (Reference: 1803.0134)

Page 227 (top and bottom) courtesy of Richard Bryant/Arcaid

Page 255 © Frank Lloyd Wright Foundation, Taliesin West, Arizona (Reference 2702.082)

Page 267 © Frank Lloyd Wright Foundation, Taliesin West, Arizona (Reference 3301.0026)

Page 269 © Frank Lloyd Wright Foundation, Taliesin West, Arizona (Reference 5213.0003)

Pages 289, 290 and 291 courtesy of Western Pennsylvania Conservancy

Page 293 courtesy of the V&A Picture Library

Page 346 courtesy of SC Johnson Company

Page 395 (top) © Frank Lloyd Wright Foundation, Taliesin West, Arizona (David Wright House – Reference 5030.0174)

Page 395 (bottom) © Frank Lloyd Wright Foundation, Taliesin West, Arizona (David Wright House – Reference 5030.0214)

Pages 410, 411 and 412 courtesy of Daniel Duhl

Pages 418 and 419 courtesy of P. Mahoney

This edition first published in 2003 by PRC Publishing Ltd, The Chrysalis Building, Bramley Road, London W10 6SP

A member of **Chrysalis** Books plc

© 2003 PRC Publishing Ltd.

ISBN 1 85648 665 6

Printed and bound in China

Contents

Introduction

Frank Lloyd Wright lived during a time of great technological advances; he saw the beginnings of the automobile and the airplane, electricity, indoor plumbing, and sanitation. He was born some thirty-six years before his namesakes, the Wright brothers, made their historic first manned flight in a machine heavier than air, and yet, within ten years of his death, Armstrong was to take his first step on the moon. Some of these great technological advances can be seen in his buildings but they are not very obvious. Wright asserted that his buildings must be first of all beautiful. "Choose the most beautiful brick (wood, stone, metal, whatever) you can afford" was his prime dictum to his clients.

Frank was born to his father's second wife, Anna Lloyd Jones, on June 8, 1867, in Richland Center, Wisconsin—due to lack of documentation, his exact birthplace is unknown. Right from the start his mother championed his cause to the detriment of everyone else, especially her husband William Cary Wright, and even her two subsequent daughters Jane and Maginel (Barney). Frank's father, William Cary Wright, was a New Englander from a family of nonconformists who had emigrated from England early on in the seventeenth century. He earned his living as a music teacher and traveling Baptist minister, until he finally settled his wife and three children at Lone Rock, Wisconsin. Money, as ever, was tight so they took in boarders, one of whom was Anna Lloyd Jones, a schoolteacher of God-fearing Unitarian Welsh stock whose wealthy land-owning family lived in Spring Green, Wisconsin.

When William was widowed in 1864 at age 44, Anna made up her mind to marry him; after all he was an attractive and intelligent man and a good catch for a strong-willed, plain, 29-year-old woman already considered over the hill by her family. Two years later, despite the age gap and their religious chasm, her family reluctantly agreed to their marriage. Within ten

Right: Frank Lloyd Wright

on

months baby Frank Lloyd Wright was born; two years later, in 1869, Jane arrived, and then nine years later, Maginel.

Frank's mother drilled into him her Unitarian values of faith in the family and a general liberal philosophy toward life. William Wright and his daughters were left in no doubt that Frank was the apple of his mother's eye and the relationship between Anna and her husband was steadily deteriorating.

Sadly, the marriage was not a success. There was no meeting of minds—William cared only for music and Anna only for education, specifically her son's education. In 1876 the young Frank Lloyd Wright experienced an important, possibly life-changing, influence. His mother went to the Centennial Exhibition in Philadelphia. Here she was enthused with the ideas of the great German educationist, Friedrich W. A. Froebel. As part of his thinking he developed the kindergarten system for very young children and, more pertinently for Frank and his mother, had developed a system of games that involved putting together simple, primary color, geometric shapes to make imaginative constructions. They were, in essence, building blocks. In his autobiography, Wright claimed that these simple toys (or "Gifts"as Froebel called them) were deeply influential and in later years he regularly cited the Froebel Gifts when talking about his approach to architecture.

Back in Wisconsin the following year, relations between his parents disintegrated further. Anna had her stepchildren sent away, and Frank had little further contact with them. Instead he got to know his cousins when he and his sister spent the summers on his uncle James Lloyd Jones's farm in Spring Green. Here, Frank found an interest in nature and the feel of the land.

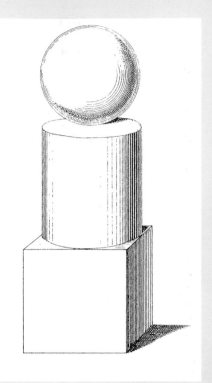

Above: Example of Froebel Gifts.

Right: Froebel Gifts illustrated in The Kindergarten Guide, *1886.*

Frank went to elementary school and high school in Madison when the Wrights moved back to Wisconsin. Frank was a somewhat lonely boy and felt that he was an outsider. When he was about fourteen and on his way home from school he encountered a group of boys tormenting a cripple, a boy who had lost both legs to polio. Frank found the courage to drive the other boys off and to help the poor unfortunate lad back up onto his crutches. Robie Lamp, the polio victim, was to become a close friend of Frank's and he spent almost as much time at Frank's house as he did at his own. Their friendship went on into adulthood, and Frank designed a small, brick house in Madison especially suited to Robie's physical needs. Frank's indignation, when aroused, would forever be marshaled to defend society's underdogs, the impoverished and downtrodden.

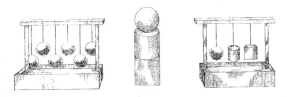

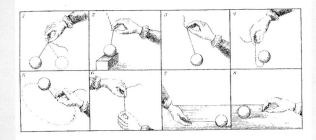

Wright's father left home when Frank was 18 and eventually divorced Anna. This left Frank completely under the influence of his fearsome mother, so much so that he became increasingly estranged from his father, even to the extent that he did not attend his funeral.

SECOND GIFT.

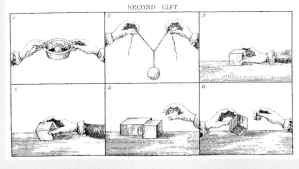

Despite his mother's intensive educational ideas and promptings, Wright failed to graduate high school and in 1885 became an apprentice to the only builder in Madison,

Allan D. Conover. As luck would have it, Conover was also the dean of engineering at the University of Wisconsin and he allowed his young apprentice to attend classes in the department of engineering. When he entered the University of Wisconsin in 1884, his interest in architecture had already declared itself. The university offered no courses in his chosen field but he gained some practical experience by working part time on a construction project at the university. Here Wright received the only strict training he got of any kind in draftsmanship, and as a junior draftsman he played a modest role in the construction of the university's Science Hall. The two years of classes he had before he dropped out showed that the young Frank had a remarkable ability of draftsmanship.

When Wright ran away from his family to Chicago (probably in late 1886) at the age of twenty he described the city as an architectural "Promised Land," the land of milk and honey. The city was being rebuilt after the fire of 1871 and he wanted to be part of the vitality pulsing through the newly constructed city. As well as being a boom town—the population doubled in every decade between 1840 and 1910—it was a progressive urban center where many new ideas were tested in architecture by new thinking on the part of the clients as well as the architects. The title "Windy City" had nothing to do with Chicago's climate. It was a somewhat derogative title bestowed upon the city by New Yorkers in reference to the "bluster" of the natives of Chicago. The city and its environs are the location for nearly one quarter of Wright's existing buildings.

Left: Frank Lloyd Wright

1886

In this year the young Frank Lloyd Wright became involved in his first architectural project, the Unity Chapel in Spring Green, Wisconsin. Wright wrote to his uncle Jenkin Lloyd Jones concerning the design of the chapel before Jones had hired Joseph Lyman Silsbee as the architect. Wright said that he had already completed some sketches for the design and was ready to alter it to meet his uncle's wishes. Given Wright's aggressive personality, even at this young stage of his life, it is possible that he was involved from the start and had contact with Silsbee during the entire design and construction phases.

Frank Lloyd Wright's home life and personal circumstances
Wright appears not to have attended the second term at the University of Wisconsin and instead may have gone to Chicago and worked for Silsbee in the middle of the year. Despite Wright's autobiography stating that he first came to Chicago in the spring of 1887, he was most likely there during the summer of 1886. He says that on his arrival in Chicago he stumbled upon a certain theatrical production of Sieba, and records show that this production was performed at Adler & Sullivan's Chicago Opera House in late August 1886.

1886 BUILDINGS

Unity Chapel, Spring Green, Wisconsin

Unity Chapel

Spring Green, Wisconsin

The chapel is open occasionally for services and during the annual Lloyd Jones family reunion.

The young Frank Lloyd Wright was allowed to oversee the construction of the Silsbee–designed chapel. Joseph Lyman Silsbee was a friend of Wright's uncle, Jenkin Lloyd Jones, a prominent Unitarian Minister for the south side of Chicago. It is not entirely clear exactly what Wright's duties were under Silsbee but if it were true that the ceiling, designed in squares, was Frank's invention then this would have been his first architectural undertaking. Wright's perspective drawing of the chapel is extraordinary for one so young but did he *design* the entire building? Recent discoveries indicate that he might well have done, albeit under the auspices of Silsbee. What we do now know is that the *Unity* magazine of August 1886 states that "a boy architect belonging to the family looked after the interior," and that it fits with his own dictum, from Lao Tse, "that it is the space within to be lived in that is the architecture, not the exterior clothing." The chapel is set in the family cemetery where many of Wright's relatives are buried along with Mamah Borthwick and some of his influential friends and associates.

Below: Unity Chapel was possibly Wright's first architectural venture.

Frank Lloyd Wright's earliest work was to some extent a deriva-
tion of the work of the leading architects of the 1880s including
H. H. Richardson, Bruce Price, and McKim, Mead & White,
whose work was widely publicized in contemporary magazines.
He was, however, both eclectic and experimental in employing
geometric forms in his earliest structures. Octagonal bays appear
in some of his plans, while semicircles and hexagonal elements
abound in his moonlighted designs.

Frank Lloyd Wright's home life and personal circumstances
When he left university in 1887, Wright moved to Chicago.
Shortly after his arrival, Wright was introduced to Joseph
Lyman Silsbee, a much sought-after architect of mainly residential buildings in the Norman Shaw "Shingle Style." Joseph
Lyman Silsbee took Wright on as an apprentice in the spring of
1887 but he soon became bored with the "safe" architecture of
Silsbee's practice and in the autumn of 1887 he moved onto
work for the firm of Adler & Sullivan where the progressive style
of their practice was much more to his taste. Louis Sullivan was
a key figure in the development of American architecture as well
as being one of the founders of the Chicago School of
Architecture. He was an articulate and poetic spokesman for
what came to be called organic architecture. This successful
integration of architectural and decorative elements influenced
a whole generation of American and European architects.

Sullivan soon saw in Wright's sketches that he was a skilled
draftsman and quickly elevated him to the position of chief of
design with thirty draftsmen working under him. Wright was his
most famous pupil and he acknowledged Sullivan as his master.
He called him "Lieber Meister," and became, as he said, "the
pencil in his (Sullivan's) hand." Sullivan was to have a profound
influence on Wright's work.

1887 BUILDINGS

**Hillside Home School,
Building I, Spring Green,
Wisconsin. (Converted to
Taliesin Fellowship com-
plex in 1933)**

PROJECTS
Misses Lloyd Jones House,
Spring Green, Wisconsin.

**Frank Lloyd Wright
writings & publications**
In August, a drawing by Wright
of Country Residence I was
published in the *Inland
Architect and News Record*.
This drawing, along with
Country Residence II, published in the same magazine
in February 1888, appeared
to be schemes for the development of Lloyd Jones family
land. The drawings are ann-
otated with the location of
Helena Valley, Wisconsin—
an area that no longer exists
but can now be found on
contemporary maps of
Wisconsin.

Hillside Home School I

Spring Green, Wisconsin

Demolished: 1950

The first Hillside Home School was built in the manner of Joseph Silsbee, who in all likelihood, also designed the nearby Unity Chapel (see 1886). The building employing the simple forms of the Shingle Style had no overhangs but, in the middle of the walls, there were two horizontal bands that ran around the school. Wright's aunts, Nell and Jane Lloyd Jones, taught in this school for many years—promising never to marry but to devote themselves instead to an educational vocation. Hillside was to become the first coeducational boarding school in the country and was noted for its progressive approach to teaching. Whenever the school needed new buildings the "aunts" never failed to call upon their nephew. In 1903, a larger structure was built. With much restructuring it eventually became part of the Taliesin Fellowship complex.

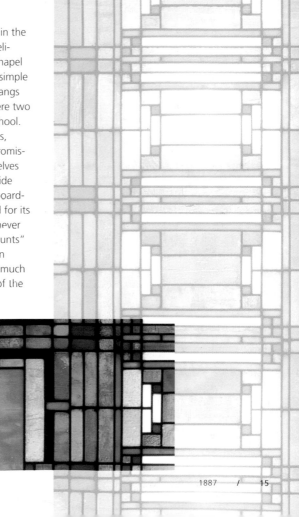

1888

Frank Lloyd Wright's home life and personal circumstances

Wright was still living with his mother and sisters who had moved to Chicago to be with him. He had started reading voraciously. The anti-establishment stance of John Ruskin, the social theorist and greatest English art and architecture critic of his time (he had championed the Pre-Raphaelites' cause) appealed to Frank, as did the progressive ideas of the Arts and Crafts Movement led by William Morris.

In June, on his twenty-first birthday, Wright purchased a corner lot at Chicago and Forest in Oak Park (next door to the house he shared with his mother and sisters) from the father of two of his early clients, Thomas and Walter Gale. This land was located across the street to the west of where Wright would build his own house a year later. The source of funds for this purchase is unknown but it may have come from his mother, Anna, who had sold the library of her late husband William Wright, and had "a little money" from the sale of her father's farm.

Frank Lloyd Wright writings & publications

In March and May two drawings by Wright were published in *Inland Architect*. They were for the J. L. Cochran and the William Waller Houses, both designed by Silsbee. In June, Wright's rendering of the Victor Falkeneau Houses, designed by Adler & Sullivan, was published in the same magazine.

Above: Plaque at the entrance doors of the Frank Lloyd Wright studio complex.

1889

Wright quickly settled into the firm of Adler & Sullivan and in 1889 signed a five-year contract. Their progressive style was much more to his taste than Silsbee's and consequently he stayed for six years. The famous contract that Wright signed in order to acquire the $5,000 to build his house was with Louis Sullivan personally and not with the firm. Louis Sullivan was a thirty-one-year-old Bostonian and already a noted architect, considered by many to be the greatest American architect of the time. His epigram "form follows function" also came to be at the heart of Wright's work. Very soon Sullivan was to design and build the world's first skyscraper, the Wainwright Building in St. Louis, Missouri. Wright greatly admired Sullivan, and was further influenced by Sullivan's personal interest in, and collection of, "Orientalia."

Frank Lloyd Wright's home life and personal circumstances

Frank married Catherine Tobin, often called "Kitty" on June 1, 1889, three months after her eighteenth birthday and within a week of Frank's twenty-second. She was the only girl and the eldest in a family of four children. The Tobins were a prosperous and socially acceptable family of Unitarians living on Chicago's fashionable south side.

For their home Wright purchased, on 5 May, the plot of land in Forest Avenue, Oak Park. The land he bought the previous year was sold just after this acquisition. With $5,000 advanced by Sullivan he set about designing and building a six-room bungalow. The building shows the influence of the "Lieber Meister" and other eastern seaboard architects such as Richardson. In common with all his houses throughout his life, this was the beginning of continuous redesigns and rebuilding.

1889 BUILDINGS

Frank Lloyd Wright Residence, Oak Park, Illinois.

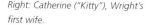
Right: Catherine ("Kitty"), Wright's first wife.

Frank Lloyd Wright Residence

951 Chicago Avenue, Oak Park, Illinois

Playroom addition with new dining room and kitchen
(1893)
Studio (1898)
Home and studio apartment conversion with garage and
caretaker's quarters (1911)
Apartment conversion altered in 1956 by Wright.
Residence, playroom, and studio restored to *c.* 1909 during
the 1970s and 1980s.
Garage converted into the Ginkgo Tree Bookshop.
Open to the public, daily tours are available.

Today, the starting point of any examination of the works of
Frank Lloyd Wright is in the first extant house of his career, his
own house and studio in Oak Park, built 1889–1909. Many
alterations were made to the original house, the most significant being the additions of the kitchen and playroom in 1893
and the studio in 1898.

As with his later homes, the architect was able to fully express his vision and the building is a monument to form, structure, and ornamentation. Wright was his own client, which meant his expression was not reserved or restricted. Ornament became one with architecture, and structure and design one with each other. The integration of Wright's home and studio—there was no separation between office and home life—reflected his involvement with the Arts and Crafts philosophy advocated by the English architect William Morris.

The original house layout, with its spacious entry, well appointed in oak, was typical of Wright's early designs. From the entry, the living room was to the left, the kitchen was straight ahead. The stairs, to the right, lead to the second floor. The dining room was in the far corner beyond the

Far left: (top) Interior of library; (bottom) home and studio exterior.

Left: Two-story drafting room.

Above: Barrel-vaulted playroom.

Left: North bedroom.

Right: Living room fireplace and inglenook.

living room. The second floor consisted of the one bedroom, bathroom, nursery, and a studio for the architect.

In the 1893 additions, Wright extended the house east from the original kitchen to create a new kitchen and gain a servant's room. A barrel-vaulted children's playroom was built above the new kitchen. A new dining room was created on the sunlit side of the house by the addition of a bay to the original kitchen. The old, original dining room became the architect's study. A low wall to create separate sleeping and dressing spaces divided the original studio upstairs. This concept of a low wall or screen rather than a partition was common in Japan and was to feature later in many of Wright's Usonian bedroom wings.

In 1898, Wright created a showpiece for his forward-thinking architectural ideas in his own studio and office at his Oak Park residence. His much-favored octagonal geometry appears throughout the plan of the library, as well as in the interlocking of square and octagon in the drafting studio. The studio was connected to the house by a passageway leading to the study. Around 1906 a complex public entry was created by a low wall that admits visitors to one or the other end of a low terrace, where they are forced to turn and enter a very narrow covered portico before arriving at the reception room proper. This created a funneling effect that eventually expanded at the main activity space—the reception room—and is typical of

Above: Stork plaque at the entrance to the studio.

Far right: Playroom looking west.

Right: Hall skylight.

much of Wright's design of entries. The reception hall is today lit by three art-glass skylights which were installed in about 1906. *The Boulders*, the two figures flanking the porch, are by Richard Bock who had a long and fruitful association with Wright.

When Wright returned to America from Europe in 1911, he remodeled the Oak Park structures into two apartments with a firewall separating the studio from the house. The original studio office became a dining room, while the two-story-high studio was split into two floors; the lower was a living room, the upper contained four bedrooms. As part of this studio conversion, a three-car garage was constructed with an additional apartment above.

The widow of the last owner of the house, Clyde Nooker, sold the property to the Home and Studio Foundation in 1974. The building now owned by the National Park Service and managed by the Home and Studio Foundation has been restored to its original state as of the year 1909, which was the last year that Wright used the house and studio as they were intended. The buildings are listed for preservation by the AIA. The Oak Park Visitor's Center is at 154 North Forest Avenue.

Far left: Dining room.

Left: Frank Lloyd Wright studio.

Overleaf: Exterior of home and studio.

1890

Wright's architecture during the 1890s was classical in nature. The decoration he was to use in these years is evidence of the influence of Louis Sullivan. With the use of the grid and a unit system in the design of his first Prairie Houses, Wright's architecture took on an immediately recognizable quality—"Prairie School architecture."

Frank Lloyd Wright's home life and personal circumstances

By this time Wright was given the majority of the domestic commissions that came to Adler & Sullivan's offices, as the principals worked on their larger, public commissions. He took sole responsibility for all domestic work handled by the firm. By now the Auditorium Building, which housed the firm, had been built—a building that made Adler & Sullivan famous from coast to coast. The building was constructed for a business syndicate to house a large civic opera house but in order to increase the income from the site it was decided to "wrap" the auditorium inside a hotel and office block. Wright was appointed head draftsman and was privileged with his own office next door to Sullivan, situated at the top of the romantic tower of the Auditorium Building itself.

Frank and Kitty's first child, Frank Lloyd Wright Jnr. (always called Lloyd), was born on March 31.

Below: Louis Sullivan Bungalow.

Louis Sullivan Bungalow

100 Holcomb Boulevard, Ocean Springs, Mississippi

Stables and Servant's Quarters.
Stables demolished, 1942.
Bungalow restored, with addition to rear and east side in
    imitation of original building, 1990.

As with the neighboring Charnley Bungalow, there is a certain controversy over who actually designed the Sullivan Bungalow, Wright or the "Lieber Meister" himself (Sullivan). What is likely, and consistent with all the known facts, is that Wright designed it in Chicago and the plans were sent to Mississippi. The basic plan is the "dog trot house" where a central breezeway separates rooms to the sides, a common layout for cottages on the Mississippi Gulf Coast. The bungalow plan had a full-width, south-facing veranda with the main entry opening to a living room, on either side of which were the guest and master bedrooms, each with its own fireplace. The plan was extended into a "T" behind the living room to accommodate the kitchen, and down the stem of the "T" was a butler's pantry, with verandas on either side, servant's quarters and a kitchen pantry. To the rear was an octagonal water tower from which Sullivan drew water for his extensive gardens. The high-pitched roof was characteristic of Wright's early work and the woodwork in the rooms remains in good condition despite the many alterations made during the restoration in the 1930s. Paneling was tongue-and-groove in local pine.

The original T-plan was altered and disfigured by the 1970 addition of a new dining room, added to the east half of the plan. But in the late 1980s, full restoration was begun by Samuel Wilson "in the style of early Wright."

The now demolished stable preserved the T-plan on a smaller scale, with kitchen and living room in the head of the "T" and carriage space and two box stalls in the stem.

1891

Wright gained a degree of recognition with his domestic commissions and his own house at Oak Park became greatly admired. Although he was only a draftsman, clients, many of them wealthy suburban businessmen and Oak Park neighbors, started coming to him personally to design and build their homes. These "bootlegged houses," as Wright called them, soon revealed an independent talent quite distinct from that of Sullivan. They were done in his own time in evenings and at weekends and holidays and didn't violate his contract with Adler and Sullivan. He was careful to keep to the letter, if not the spirit, of his contract. Such work proved a great financial boon as Wright's family was proving cripplingly expensive.

1891 BUILDINGS

James Charnley House, Chicago, Illinois.

W. S. MacHarg House, Chicago, Illinois.

Right: Charnley House stairwell.

Below: Charnley House carved interior decoration.

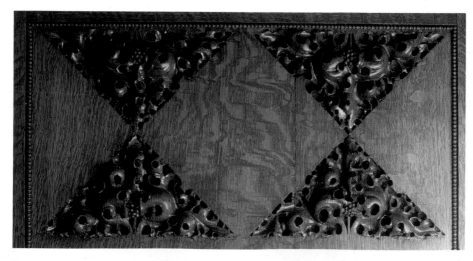

James Charnley House

1365 North Astor Street, Chicago, Illinois

House can be seen from the street.
Tours by appointment only.

James Charnley owned a lumber company and was a friend of
Louis Sullivan. Wright was still working for Adler & Sullivan at
the time of the construction of this house but the story is that
he was given the job to design this residence as the firm was
concentrating on commercial commissions. Wright called this
town house "the first modern building" and in it, he said, he
first recognized the decorative value of plain surfaces. This residence clearly shows Wright's early promise and is a confident,
elegantly structured work.

The plan of the house is simple, a rectangle broken by a
dining room bay on the south. A finely carved, woodwork stairwell is also a sky-lit atrium, which rises to the top of the building
and is flanked on each floor by two rooms. The kitchen, as was
the norm for town houses built on city lots with limited space,
was located in the basement. The style and simplicity of the
Charnley House, built symmetrically about an east-west axis,
was ahead of its time in terms of the way the exterior reflects
interior space and is, in reality, the first great building of
Wright's career. The house does, nevertheless, owe a great deal
to Sullivan. The open second-story loggia was a favorite device
of Sullivan's, as were the arches inside and on the ground
floor—six in all—but perhaps the most Sullivanesque touches
are in the decorative detailing on the wood trim throughout the
house. Later additions squared off the dining-room bay window.

The Chicago architectural firm of Skidmore, Owings &
Merrill purchased the house in 1986, making it their headquarters. Restoration, completed in 1988 by John A. Eifler, reveals a
living room with Wright's choice of American white oak and a
dining room with Sullivan's Mexican (Tabasco) mahogany. The

original brick has darkened from a lighter orange, having been sprayed with linseed oil, a common masonry sealant of the 1890s and new brick on the south facade has been similarly sealed.

Above: Charnley House carved interior decoration.

Left: Charnley House facade.

1892

The contract that Wright had signed with Louis Sullivan in 1889 contained no provisions pertaining to outside work, sometimes termed "moonlighting." In fact it should have been to Sullivan's advantage to allow Wright to work outside the office in order for him to repay the $5,000 loan. The interest on the loan was high and Wright's wages alone for Adler & Sullivan would have made the repayments difficult.

Frank Lloyd Wright's home life and personal circumstances
Frank and Kitty's second son, John, was born.

1892 BUILDINGS CONTINUED

Warren McArthur House, Chicago, Illinois. (*Above and right.*)

R. P. Parker House, Oak Park, Illinois. (*Opposite.*)

Albert Sulllivan House, Chicago, Illinois, site.

George Blossom House

4858 Kenwood Avenue, Chicago, Illinois

The house can be seen from the street.

This "bootlegged" house with its yellow clapboard siding, white trim, classical portico, fan-lighted doorway, and Palladian windows appears to be a classic example of New England Colonial Revival architecture. A closer study, however, reveals the modern innovations that Wright introduced. The low hip roof, the projection of the eaves (which replace the traditional classical cornice), and the massive Roman brick chimney are pure Wright. The interior of the house contrasts with the conventional style of the exterior.

With the exception of the conservatory at the rear, the plan is essentially symmetrical, with the living room at the center of the house, the staircase on the north side, and a Palladian window on the south side. Stairs to a covered porch, then passing

Below: Blossom House exterior.

into a narrow anteroom, gains entry. To the left is a parlor, straight ahead is a double-banded archway framing the fireplace inglenook beyond, and to the right is a dead-end reception room. A formal dining room is situated beyond the dining room on the south, while on the north side of the dining room is the stairwell protected by a balustrade of recti-linear balusters. The house includes a separate servant's stair to the half-level landing, a fea-ture common in much of Wright's pre-Prairie homes. This allowed the servant to go upstairs unseen. The third level is a full-length studio in balloon construction. The archways in the building reflect Sullivan's influence on Wright but there are many more features of the house that are purely Wrightian, including the bead-ed board siding and the patterned leaded-glass windows. Today, built-in seating has been removed from the conservatory but the home is generally in excellent condition.

The contrasting Prairie Style garage, built at a later date (1907), was complete with a turntable, grease pits, and a chauffeur's resi-dence upstairs. Today it has been renovated as a single, family residence.

Above right: Blossom House dining room.

Right: Blossom House entrance.

Above, left, and far left: Details of windows from Blossom House.

1893

In 1893, Frank was exposed to two more crucial influences on his development as an architect when the World's Columbian Exposition was held in Chicago to mark the 400th anniversary of the discovery of America by Columbus. The first was pre-Columbian architecture, as represented by the replica of the Mayan nunnery at Uxmal. It is possible that the influence of pre-Columbian and Mayan architectural forms and motifs in Wright's early work was influenced by what he observed here. The other influence was Japanese culture. Already aware and intrigued with Oriental art, the latter caught his imagination in the form of a half-scale replica of a wooden temple from the Fujiwara period. His interest in Japanese architecture was probably also kindled by one of the most popular exhibits, The Ho-o-den, a wooden temple erected on a small plot of land set in an artificial lake.

One of Wright's most important architectural innovations can be traced back to the Ho–o-den. In his Prairie Houses, he abandoned the conventional "box" containing smaller "boxes" created by fixed interior dividing walls. Wright also saw that the most efficient place to support a roof was not at its very edges but slightly in at the corners, thereby allowing the roof to create a large overhang.

Frank Lloyd Wright's home life and personal circumstances

Inevitably Sullivan found out about Wright's "bootlegged" houses and, predictably, was not impressed with Wright's explanations. They parted company after a furious row and were not reconciled for twenty years. However, in 1924, Wright wrote Sullivan's definitive obituary. The row between Wright and Sullivan may not be the only reason Wright left the firm. There was a depression that began in the spring of 1893 and deepened as the summer wore on. A note published about the condition of Adler & Sullivan indicated that there were only three employees left by August and, outside the firm, Wright had won a competition to design two boathouses in Madison, Wisconsin.

Immediately after quitting the firm, Wright and his friend Cecil Corwen rented space in the tower of the Schiller building but the partnership soon ended when Corwen moved back east.

Wright met Daniel H. Burnham, partner in the firm of Burnham & Root, and, as the new president of the AIA, the chief organizer of the great Chicago World's Fair. His company was a rival architectural firm to Adler & Sullivan in Chicago and Frank courageously turned down a very generous offer made to him by Burnham. His instincts correctly told him the position would lead him in the wrong direction to a possible dead end.

Together with several other young architects, Frank set up his own practice in Steinway Hall, Chicago. The work flowed in and he was able to build up a successful, if unremarkable, business doing "period" homes for local clients, again many of them his Oak Park neighbors. These comfortably well-off men invariably spent more on their houses than they had originally intended —especially if Wright designed the furniture and fittings for the interiors, as was his wont.

Left: Goan House

Walter M. Gale House

1031 Chicago Avenue, Oak Park, Illinois

The house can be seen from the street.

In October 1891, Thomas Gale bought his father's (Edwin O. Gale) six residential lots on Chicago Avenue. By June 6, 1892, a Mr. Beman and his wife bought this lot but by October 1893 they had sold the property back to the Gales—to Thomas's brother, Walter, a bachelor who worked as a druggist in downtown Chicago. It was Walter Gale who had Wright design the house as it is today and it is arguably the most interesting and gracious of the three early homes that the architect designed for Chicago Avenue. The design with its spindle railing and open porch is unique to Wright's early work as most of the Prairie buildings had porches with roofs, which were integrated into the buildings. The three-story turret, however, is reminiscent of Joseph Silsbee (see Unity Chapel in 1886). The huge polygonal windows in this house are evidence of Wright's increasing interest in the ways in which rooms could be "opened up" to the outside and nature.

Right and below: Walter M. Gale House exterior.

The rather grand entry hall faces to the side, not the street, and has beaded-edge wood paneling. From the entry hall one can turn left into the dead-end reception room, move ahead to the library (which today would be a living room), turn right to a door leading to the kitchen, or turn around to the stairs. The dormer rises from the second floor, where closets, to the third story, frame it.

Walter Gale sold the property in March 1906. The original front terrace, long since destroyed, was restored in 1977. New owners of the property, Vicki and Kenneth Prouty, continued restoration into the late 1980s.

1894

Frank Lloyd Wright's home life and personal circumstances

Catherine Wright Baxter, the eldest daughter of Frank and his wife Kitty, was born early in the year. She was headstrong like her father. She was the mother of Anne Baxter, the late film star and actress.

1894 BUILDINGS

Frederick Bagley House, Hillsdale, Illinois.

H. W. Basset House (remodeling), Oak Park, Illinois.

Robert W. Roloson Row Houses, Chicago, Illinois.

William Herman Winslow House, River Forest, Illinois.

Francis Wooley House, Oak Park, Illinois.

PROJECTS

Concrete Monolithic Bank

Orris Goan House, LaGrange, Illinois.

McAfee House, Chicago, Illinois.

Frank Lloyd Wright writings & publications

The Architect and the Machine was the first of many papers and writings in which Wright would expound his theories. It was Wright's first essay on architecture that he read it to the University Guild at Evanston, Illinois. In his radically original designs, as well as in his prolific writings, he championed the virtues of what he termed "organic architecture," a building style based on natural forms. He formulated six design principles that defined organic architecture:

First principle: the measures of art were simplicity and repose. Everything that was unnecessary—including interior dividing walls—had to be eliminated, while details like decoration, fixtures, and furniture were to be integrated into the overall structure.

Second principle: called for as many different styles of houses as there were "styles" of people. Designs could provide each client with a house that expressed their individuality and architects no longer had to rely on the historical styles that had dominated nineteenth-century architecture.

Third principle: linked together nature, the landscape or the building site, and the architecture. Buildings should appear to "grow" from the site and should be shaped to harmonize with their surroundings.

Fourth principle: the colors of buildings should be derived from nature and should be adapted to harmonize with the building materials.

Fifth principle: concerns the expression of the "nature of the materials." Each material should show its natural texture, grain, and color and not be "disguised" to look like another material.

Sixth principle: expressed Wright's belief that buildings should have qualities that were analogous to the human qualities of truth, sincerity, and beauty and that buildings should bring people joy.

Robert Roloson Row Houses

3213-3219 Calumet, Chicago, Illinois

The houses can be seen from the street.

Robert M. Roloson was the son-in-law of Edward C. Waller, marrying his daughter in 1894. Roloson purchased four row houses, set on three 25-foot-wide city lots, and commissioned Wright to remodel them.

This commission was the first of Wright's "apartment" projects and as the only built example of city row houses they are unique to the architect. The idea was to erect a row of four identical houses to be rented out and provide a return on the client's investment. The modified Tudor style houses were conceived on a mezzanine plan. There is a break in the floor level at the central stairwell and the rooms to the rear of the stairs are several steps lower than the ones at the front. Interior spaces constantly shift as the floor heights vary and the main rooms are separated from each other by smaller "introductory" rooms. The front exterior of the Roloson Houses is dominated by the four great gables and the only applied ornament is in the three square spandrels on each facade. A flight of three steps approaches a paved terrace in front of each house and separating the terraces from the sidewalk are balustrades decorated with Sullivanesque patterns. A second scheme appears in the drawings, but it is not clear if this was a later remodeling of the same building or a rethinking during its construction. In 1981, despite having been designated a Chicago Landmark, the interiors were gutted after deterioration and fire. The present interiors are a pale imitation of Wright's artistic originals but the brown brick exterior is noted for its abstract stone work similar to Sullivan's early period. It was Wright's intention to have the gables removed but this was never carried out.

William Herman Winslow House

515 Auvergne Place, River Forest, Illinois

The front of the house can be seen from the street.

This was Wright's first important independent commission after he left Adler & Sullivan and represents a major breakthrough in his career. It is a demonstration of his early mastery of classical form and hints at the Prairie Houses to come. The dichotomy of the simple street facade and the more complex rear of the house, with its projecting wing and tall polygonal stair-tower, is a result of the architect's design methods. The house was planned and then the floor plan was made to fit. On the north side of the house is an elegant porte-cochere, with parking space beneath, and the spandrel of the arched structure are carved in leafy motifs reminiscent of Sullivan.

The house suggests an influence from the Turkish exhibition building that was shown at the 1893 World Columbian Exposition. The classical base-column-capital motif demonstrates

the extent to which Wright understood classicism and the design tenets of the time. Certain stylistic characteristics were to stay with the architect throughout his life—the stylobate-like foundation that firmly sets the house on the earth, the first-floor living quarters that dominate the structure, the low, hipped-roof above broad overhanging eaves, and, in two-story structures, the second story that is like a gallery, never dominating the first floor. The house has a full basement and a finished attic floor for servants. The double-hung windows used here are a rarity among Wright's Prairie and later designs, where casement windows were the norm.

The basic material is tapestry brick of Roman dimensions while stone and plaster (in the frieze, which is not terra-cotta) are also employed. When Wright first built the roof, the frieze nearly matched the color of the brick and so the house was monochromatic—the limestone trim was not painted white. The trim around the front door, however, is much more severe and abstract than both the plaster frieze, which surrounds the second story, and the oak carving on top of the front entry door. The influence of Louis Sullivan is again evident where the masonry elements are treated to a foliage ornament. The front door opens directly to a hall with a fireplace set behind ornate columns and, typically, Wright establishes the hearth as the focus of the domestic scene.

Left and above: The simple facade contrasts with the more complex design of the rear of the house with its projecting wing and polygonal tower.

This house has been designated by the American Institute of Architects as one of the seventeen American buildings designed by Wright to be retained as an example of his architectural contribution to American culture.

1895

Two clients of Wright, Chauncey Willams, and William Winslow, joined forces in 1895 to found a small publishing firm, the Auvergne Press, which Wright joined as chief designer. This was also the year that Marion Mahony, only the second woman to receive a degree in architecture from the Massachusetts Institute of Technology, joined Wright's Oak Park studio and became indispensable as his delineator. Some of the designs for interior furnishings, mosaics, stained glass, and murals for which Wright took complete credit are now thought to have been created by Mahony.

Wright found that he increasingly liked working from home so he built himself a separate studio at his house, where he could concentrate on his work away from his large family.

1895 BUILDINGS

Francis Apartments, Chicago, Illinois.

Francisco Terrace Apartments, Chicago, Illinois. (*Right.*)

Nathan G. Moore House (rebuilt after fire in 1923), Oak Park, Illinois.

Below: Waller Apartments.

1895 BUILDINGS CONTINUED

**Edward C. Waller Apartments,
Chicago, Illinois.**

**Chauncey L. Williams House,
River Forest, Illinois.**
(*Above and right.*)

**H.R. Young House, Oak Park,
Illinois**

PROJECTS

Amusement Park, Wolf Lake,
Illinois.

Baldwin House, Oak Park,
Illinois.

Lexington Terrace Apartment
Building, Chicago, Illinois.

Luxfer Prism Company
Skyscraper, Chicago, Illinois.

Nathan G. Moore House

Residence remodeling (1923)
Stable (1923)
The house can be seen from the street. Open to the public.
    Guided tours available during summer months.

Originally from Pennsylvania, Moore became a lawyer in Peoria before moving to Chicago.

Nathan Moore had asked Wright for an "English House" and it transpired that he wanted a mock Tudor, half-timbered black and white house. The result was a cross-gabled, Roman-brick, half-timbered house that was imitated by architects for years to come. At first Wright contemplated the idea of simply remodeling Moore's existing old-frame house in Forest Avenue, directly opposite his own studio. Although elaborate plans (now lost) were drawn up the idea was abandoned. Moore House II was completed in 1895.

The top floor and roof of the house were rebuilt after a fire gutted the building on Christmas Day, 1922. Wright was commissioned for the rebuilding and the new enlarged Moore House II was built on the same foundations, with the result that the outward appearance of the present building relates more to the architect's house designs of the late 1920s, although the original form has been retained. The steeply pitched roof was made even more dramatic by extending the roof downward,

Left: The design of the Moore House was imitated by architects for years to come.

from just above the second-floor window lintels to the first-floor lintel line. Chimneys were enlarged, the tile roof was replaced by slate, and the horizontal trim was removed so that the vertical nature of the structure was emphasized.

The redesign was much more decorative than the earlier work and included a considerable amount of terra cotta with its carved brick and stonework. Wright also built the stable and garage to the west of the south yard.

To complicate matters the original frame building that Wright had earlier contemplated remodeling was moved to the south edge of the property to make room for the first Moore House II. In 1900, the original frame building was remodeled and still stands. It is known as Moore House III.

Left and below: Side elevation and porch of the Moore House.

1896

C. R. Ashbee was a British architect who founded the Guild of Handicrafts that had distinct resemblances to Wright's Taliesin Fellowship. Ashbee was a gifted designer and a devoted follower of William Morris, the acknowledged leader of the Arts and Crafts Movement as it evolved in Britain in the 1880s, and his tireless willingness to travel and lecture made him a natural leader when Morris died in 1896. This was the year that Ashbee and Wright met, while the former was making his first trip to the United States. Ashbee was one of the first European enthusiasts for Wright's work.

1896 BUILDINGS

Harry C. Goodrich House, Oak Park, Illinois. (*Right.*)

Isidore Heller House, Chicago, Illinois.

Romeo and Juliet Windmill Tower, Spring Green, Wisconsin.

Charles E. Roberts House, Oak Park, Illinois.

George W. Smith House, Oak Park, Illinois.

PROJECTS

Devin House, Chicago, Illinois.
Perkins Apartment, Chicago, Illinois.
Roberts Houses (four houses), Ridgeland, Illinois.

Isidore Heller House

5132 Woodlawn Avenue, Chicago, Illinois

The house can be seen from the street.

The Heller House is a long and narrow L-plan of rectangular interlocking spaces with a "monitor" roof. A third story is added above the main eaves and is capped with its own roof. It is among the earliest of Wright's three-story residence designs. The primary axis of the house is east west, with its entry on the south side rather than on the street facade. Although Wright often used this arrangement to gain southern exposure, in this case it was dictated by the narrowness of the lot.

The main door of the house is a square opening, flanked on either side by Romanesque columns. Above the entrance, at the second story level, is an inset porch with a row of filigreed terra-cotta columns that support the load above. The large house was planned with four sizeable bedrooms and a small room as a servant's quarters, with the living room occupying the front quarter of the house. The main hallway runs from the center of the living room past the entry and reception room (with stairs on the opposite side) to the fireplace at the end of the dining room. To the rear are a kitchen and the servants' dining room. The third floor of the house was to contain a playroom.

The interior features waxed white oak with plaster "saturated with pure color" in a rough sand finish. The exterior of the house is of yellow Roman brick with two-toned brick used on the second and third story, which is only partly enclosed and has a frieze decorated with

figures by Richard Bock, a sculptor who Wright worked with on several of his commissions. Bock's human figures, carved in high relief, are the central feature of each panel of the frieze.

It is conceivable that the use of stiff, colonial cames in Wright's art glass first appeared in this house and it is possible that William Winslow's patented technique for setting glass in metal was used in the stair hall windows.

Left and inset: The house is distinguished by the addition of a "monitor."

Romeo and Juliet Windmill Tower

Spring Green, Wisconsin

The windmill is visible from several vantage points and tours are occasionally available from the Visitors' Center.

Wright's aunts, Nell and Jane Lloyd Jones, wanted a windmill built to complete their new water system beside the reservoir, dug out of solid rock, on top of the hill above the Hillside Home School. The aunts were all for letting Frank design something new and he produced a sixty-foot wooden tower of a most radical and unusual design. The windmill was composed of an interlocking diamond and octagon, representing Shakespeare's lovers Romeo and Juliet embracing (and structurally supporting) each other. It was capped by a disc and contained a circular staircase. It stood on a stone-and-concrete base, reinforced horizontally by a wooden platform every ten feet and clad in shingles, to match the building he had constructed for the aunts some ten years earlier. The windmill was resurfaced in 1938 with horizontal cypress board-and-batten siding.

Wright's uncles were opposed to the structure from the start and claimed that it would not last the first storm. Ironically, it has remained standing in its present form for nearly a century, a fact that is generally attributed to the bracing floors inside, and the membrane skin outside.

As the windmill aged, Wright himself tried at one point to save it by pouring concrete into the structure halfway to its top. Several later attempts at restoration failed until, in 1990, serious efforts led to scaffolding and fund-raising ventures. The windmill was torn down and a new structure was erected on the original stone base and capped with the roof saved from the original structure. In 1992, two days before the celebration at Taliesin of the 125th anniversary of Frank's birth, a new Romeo and Juliet was dedicated.

Left: The windmill was a radical design with interlocking diamond and octagon shapes that represented the lovers embracing.

Frank Lloyd Wright's home life and personal circumstances
Frank Lloyd Wright moved his architectural practice to Oak Park.

1897 BUILDINGS

George Furbeck House, Oak Park, Illinois. (*Below and right.*)

Rollin Furbeck House, Oak Park, Illinois.

Mrs Thomas H. Gale Summer House, Whitehall, Michigan.

PROJECTS
All Souls Building, Lincoln Center, Chicago, Illinois.
Chicago Screw Company Factory Building, Chicago, Illinois.

Rollin Furbeck House

515 Fair Oaks Avenue, Oak Park, Illinois

Residence Remodelling (1907)
The house can be seen from the street.

This three-storied house was built by Wright at the behest of stockbroker Warren Furbeck as a wedding present for his son Rollin. Rollin kept the house for only a year before moving on.

The house is essentially a square plan with first-floor extensions—open porches at the north half of the front and rear facades and a porte-cochere on the south at the rear. The house represents a major transitional work, from early square and rectangular plans to the Prairie cruciform and pinwheel designs of Wright's first mature design period. "This first emphatically

forward-looking design excites with its remarkable experimentation. The towering central pavilion makes it even taller on an elevated site. The very open picture window on the first floor contrasts sharply with the recessed diamond-paned windows above." (Quoted from Alice Sinkevitch's *AIA Guide to Chicago*).

The house has a light tan brick and colored wood trim facade. The upper-story windows hug the broad overhanging eaves of the hipped roof in a band of stucco. There are two design trends evident in this structure: firstly, the brick base rising to the second-floor sills, Bedford limestone trim, window symmetry, broad hip roofs, central chimney, and porte-cochere; secondly, a central three-story mass with decorative columns. The picture windows in the living and dining rooms represent the first residential use of this architectural element and the building also features one of the last of Wright's square semi-detached entry porches. The architect also employed another favorite device, running the surface of a lower floor to the sills of the next higher floor, at both the second and third levels.

The staircase to the north of the gallery connects entry, living room, and kitchen and turns toward the center of the north wall to reach the second floor. A half-level bathroom is located under the stairwell in what would otherwise have been stairs to the basement—the true basement staircase is at the rear of the kitchen. As there is a bathroom in the third-floor "attic" this area was probably used as servants' quarters. The house appears to exhibit Wright's first use of cantilevering in domestic design. Part of a rear room is cantilevered well beyond the second-floor exterior wall structural support. This technique was to become common in the architect's later Prairie structures.

During the restoration of the property, begun in the mid-1980s by Linda and William Ryan, much was learned of the original nature of the house. Exterior restoration has included a new wood-shingled roof, single-beaded copper gutters and downspouts, and chemical stripping of paint from exterior masonry and plaster columns.

Above: Rollin Furbeck house living room.

Left: Rollin Furbeck house entrance.

1898

Frank Lloyd Wright's home life and personal circumstances
Frances Wright Cuppley, the youngest daughter of Frank and his first wife Catherine, was born.

1898 BUILDINGS

River Forest Golf Club, site.

PROJECTS
Mozart Gardens Restaurant remodeling, Chicago, Illinois.

River Forest Golf Club

River Forest, Illinois

Additions and alterations (1901)
Demolished

This was the only clubhouse Wright designed in this early period but it acted as a prototype of several to come. This single-story structure of horizontal board-and-batten siding was possibly the earliest known major work of Wright's to employ this surfacing. The original structure was nothing more than a porch, an assembly room, and men and women's lounges set behind a fireplace.

A large octagonal common room, enlarged in 1901 with a fireplace on either side behind the original fireplace, was the central feature of the building. Wings extended forward and sideways from this central space, turning back on themselves with open terraces at both ends enclosing two small courtyards. These side wings provided expanded men's locker rooms on one side and a dining room on the other. A kitchen was attached to the dining room and caretaker's quarters to the lockers. Characterized by its ribbon windows, bands of masonry and shingle, and very low, widely overhanging hip roofs, the River Forest Clubhouse was the nearest Wright got to the Prairie House in this early period of his work.

1899

1899 BUILDINGS

Joseph Husser House, Chicago, Illinois.

Edward C. Waller House (Gatehouse and Gardener's Cottage, 1901), River Forest, Illinois.

PROJECTS
Cheltenham Beach Resort, near Chicago, Illinois.
Eckhart House, River Forest, Illinois.

Joseph and Helen Husser House

730 (was 180) Buena Avenue, Chicago, Illinois

Demolished: 1923 or 1924

The Husser House was a forerunner of the Prairie House, and the last commission where the influence of Louis Sullivan on ornamentation would be so apparent. Its subsequent demolition represents a notable loss. As with the Prairie Houses, the houses of Wright's "First Golden Age" with their living quarters above ground level, this building had the basement at ground level with the house rising two stories higher, as much as anything for protection from flooding by nearby Lake Michigan. The building's centrifugal plan—a forerunner of the "pinwheel" and "windmill" plans of later works—was typical Prairie Style. By placing the basement at ground level it ceased to be a basement but became an area for "secondary activities" in the house, such as laundry areas, servant's rooms, entry halls, or children's play areas. The elevated positions of the dining room and living rooms gave them open views across the landscape – in this case Lake Michigan The bedrooms in Husser House were located on the third story, corresponding to where the attics would normally have been. This brought about an increased horizontality because the house did not have to accommodate any additional height under its roof. The whole three-story building was lower in height than the more usual two-and-a-half story houses.

Joseph Husser was an official in the Christian Science Church and was an executive for a real-estate broker. He bought this site from James B. Waller and lived in the house until 1923. The furniture designed by Wright was saved and the dining room (complete with table and chairs) was auctioned in 1987 making $1.6 million.

1900

By 1900 Wright's architectural style had matured and he built Bradley House and Hickox House in Kankakee, Illinois. This was really the start of what has been called Wright's "First Golden Age," which extended into the 1910s. In this phase he created a distinctly American house type—the Prairie House—characterized by a strong horizontality, a use of natural materials, and close attention to the links between the building and its site. The designs feature consistent use of a grid composed of squares, most often centered on door and window mullions. Within this grid, a unit system provided Wright a method with which to express both a coherent vision of American architecture as well as his own strong ideals.

The Prairie era emerged from various experiments in the nineties in which Wright developed his own style. He would build over thirty houses during the next decade.

Frank Lloyd Wright writings & publications

The Architect published in *The Brickbuilder* (June).
Here, in his second address to the Architectural League, Wright decried the fate of American architecture. He blamed its lack of integrity directly on the pressures commerce was exerting over the architect and says that the profession of architecture had begun degenerating before the turn of the century and was continuing in its misguided pursuit of direction. In the article Wright lays the groundwork for a solution based on the proper education of the architect.

1900 BUILDINGS

Jessie M. Adams House, Chicago, Illinois.

B. Harley Bradley House "Glenlloyd," Kankakee, Illinois.

S. A. Foster House, Chicago, Illinois.

Warren Hickox House, Kankakee, Illinois.

Fred B. Jones House "Penwern," Boathouse and Gate Lodge, Lake Delavan, Wisconsin.

E. H. Pitkin Lodge, Desbarats, Ontario, Canada.

Henry Wallis Summer House (Gatehouse remodeled: 1901), Lake Delavan, Wisconsin. (*Right.*)

PROJECTS
Abraham Lincoln Center,
    Chicago, Illinois.
Francis W. Little House I, Peoria,
    Illinois.
Motion Picture Theater, Los
    Angeles, California.
School, Crosbytown, Texas.

Left: Wallis House

Fred B. Jones Residence, "Penwern"

3335 South Shore Drive, Lake Delavan, Wisconsin

Boathouse
Gate Lodge with water tower and greenhouse (1901)
Barn with stables (1901)
Major addition to the south corner of the house; rear
    porch altered. Greenhouse demolished. Barn altered.
    Boathouse destroyed by fire, 1975. Water tower torn
    down.
Gate Lodge visible from the road, house only visible from
    the lake. The grounds are private.

This is the most extensive of the Lake Delavan Projects. In the main building, distinctive arches at the porte-cochere and front veranda distinguish it from all the other lakeside cottages. The architectural features of the house are unusual for Wright's work during this period, but are similar to those he had produced previously. It has been suggested that the house was designed four or five years earlier and there was a substantial delay before work commenced on the site.

The interior features a large, back-to-back Roman brick fireplace that serves both the dining room and the living room. The living room runs the width of the lakefront facade with the veranda surrounding it on three sides. The fourth side of the living room is a central entry with a staircase leading to a balcony that overlooks it and other rooms. There is only one bathroom for the five bedrooms but one bedroom, along with the billiards room behind the kitchen, has its own fireplace. In 1921 a large two-story addition, built on the southwest, and an alteration to the rear porch destroyed the building's proportions. The exterior of board-and-batten siding was originally stained but is now painted.

The gate lodge, with a furnace and coal bin, was originally equipped for year-round living and had four bedrooms plus a bathroom above the living, dining, and kitchen facilities. The lodge was connected to a water tower via the gateway to the main residence, and a greenhouse (since demolished) extended into the property from the tower.

Fred B. Jones treated this residence very much as a summer retreat for his work colleagues until his death in 1934. When he died his will was contested by his relatives and a bank took control of the entire property, which lay empty for five years, until it was purchased by Burr Robbins, who lived there for nearly fifty years. Today the house and the gatehouse are separately owned.

Right: The living room runs the width of the lakefront facade and is surrounded by a veranda on three sides.

1901

Although nobody at the time took up Wright's revolutionary approach to flexible, open-plan living, it attracted much attention and brought him to a public beyond Illinois and Wisconsin. In time, this innovative concept came to be considered his earliest major contribution to modern architecture and was the germ of his Prairie Houses. Also this year, in the magazine *The Brickbuilder*, Wright published his design for his monolithic bank building in concrete. In his version of the bank, Wright let the cast concrete become the aesthetic of the building, much as he would do more eloquently in the Unity Temple three years later.

1901 BUILDINGS

E. Arthur Davenport House, River Forest, Illinois. (*Right and left.*)

William G. Fricke House, Oak Park, Illinois.

F. B. Henderson House, Elmhurst, Illinois.

River Forest Golf Club additions, Illinois.

Frank Wright Thomas House, Oak Park, Illinois.

Frank Lloyd Wright writings & publications

A Home in a Prairie Town, was the first of two articles Wright was commissioned to write for the *Ladies' Home Journal* (February 3) that brought him to more than just parochial architectural attention. His project was to develop a comfortable home for about $7,000.

The other article for the journal (July 8) was entitled *A Small House with Lots of Room in It.*

The Art and Craft of the Machine was published in the catalogue of the fourteenth annual exhibition of the Chicago Architectural Club (March). This article was both a defense of the Arts and Craft Movement in Britain and and a critique of those exhibiting an out-and-out hostility to machine production:

"Is it not more likely that the medium of artistic expression itself has broadened and changed until a new definition and new direction must be given the art-activity of the future, and that the Machine has finally made for the artist, whether he will yet own it or not a splendid distinction between the Art of old and the Art to come? A distinction made by the tool which frees human labor, lengthens and broadens the life of the simplest man, thereby the basis of the Democracy upon which we insist."

Edward C. Waller Gatehouse and Gardener's Cottage, River Forest, Illinois.

Ward W. Willits House, Highland Park, Illinois.

Ward W. Willits Gardener's Cottage with Stables (remodeled into house), Highland Park, Illinois.

Above left: Fricke House.

Below left: Thomas House.

Right: Thomas House.

Ward W. Willits House

1445 Sheridan Road, Highland Park, Illinois

Private property; the front of the house can be seen from
the street.

Wright's Prairie House design incorporated large, free flowing
living areas, well lit by windows that opened the house to continuous views of the grounds. The Willits House is the first great
house of Wright's Prairie period and is an important building
because it shows the culmination of all Wright's feelings about
residential architecture with the furnishings designed specifically
for the stylish interior. Gone are any suggestions of Tudor half-
timber trim. The building presents a formal, almost symmetrical,
facade to the street, establishing the precedent for houses with
symmetrical wings. The rooflines present a reasonably balanced

*Below: The Willits House is a fine
example of Wright's Prarie Style.*

Left: The dark wood trim and stucco surface is a hallmark of the Prarie Style.

Below: The exterior is composed of a series of vertical and horizontal interlocking planes.

cruciform with the dining room offset, providing more space than could be achieved in a square or rectangular layout. The long, low-roofed porte-cochere at the front entrance balances the low-roofed porch at the end of the dining room. Each wing of the house comes off a central core in a pinwheel configuration. The end wall of the living room is floor-to-ceiling glass, open to the yard, to nature, across a large terrace. On the sides, high windows concentrate the view away from the ground and upward to the sky.

Inside the house, oak is used on the main floor, pine above, and stringcourses are used on both floors. The core of the building is a substantial, Roman brick, central fireplace—"the physical and spiritual center of the home" from which each wing of the house extends. Behind the kitchen are a flight of service stairs, two servants' bedrooms, and a bathroom. Off a narrow corridor on the second floor are three fitted bedrooms, two further bathrooms, and a large nursery. The main staircase

Below: High windows concentrate the view upward to the sky.

of the house rises through the double height space; a library is on the landing with a small reception room on the floor below. The building is constructed from wood and steel with exterior plasterwork and wood trim and the living quarters are all raised above ground level by a chunky stylobate, typifying true Prairie Style. Wright also designed a gardener's cottage and stables behind the house.

Willits became chairman of the board of Adams & Westlake Brass & Bronze Foundry, the company that originally employed Orlando Giannini—Wright's main art-glass supplier for some years and it was probably Gianni who provided the connection between client and architect. Ward Willits lived in the house until his death in 1952 at the age of ninety-two. The house has been sensitively restored and relandscaped by its current owners and is designated by the AIA as one of seventeen American buildings designed by Wright to be retained as an example of his architectural contribution to American culture.

Below: This exterior view shows the long, low-roofed porte-cochère (on the right) and the dining room (on the left).

1902

1902 BUILDINGS

Walter Gerts Duplex, Whitehall, Michigan.

George Gerts Cottage, Whitehall, Michigan.

Herbert House, Evanston, Illinois.
 Asbury Avenue
 Davis Street

Arthur Heurtley House, Oak Park, Illinois. (*Right and below.*)

Arthur Heurtley Cottage, Marquette Island, Michigan.

Hillside Home School Building II, Spring Green, Wisconsin.

Lake Delavan Yacht Club, Lake Delavan, Wisconsin.

1902 BUILDINGS CONTINUED

Francis W. Little House I, Peoria, Illinois. (*Opposite and below.*)

Living room, Metropolitan Museum of Art, New York City, New York (1982)

William Martin House, Oak Park, Illinois.

Charles Ross House, Lake Delavan, Wisconsin.

George Spencer House, Lake Delavan, Wisconsin.

PROJECTS
Metzger House, Ontario, Canada.
Waller House I, Charlevoix, Michigan.
Yahara Boat Club, Madison, Wisconsin.

Hillside Home School II

Spring Green, Wisconsin

Converted in 1933 to the Taliesin Fellowship Complex. Tours arranged through the Taliesin Visitors' Center.

Wright's mother's sisters, aunts Jane and Nell, had conceived of the Hillside Home School established in "The Valley" in 1886. The school took children of all ages from kindergarten through high school. When Unity Chapel opened the aunts used it as a temporary school while they built larger quarters. This was the second school building Wright designed (the first being in 1897) and was constructed in the manner of Joseph Lyman Silsbee, who designed the nearby Unity Chapel. The building is rose-colored sandstone with oak beams, capped by a red tile roof.

   Two cruciform units comprise the main part of the school, a gymnasium dominating the west wing and a three-story assembly room with gallery to the right, and classrooms linking the wings. Rooms to the north of the assembly room are linked by a bridge-gallery over the driveway.

   The school was altered after a second-floor fire and went on to become successful for many years. By 1907 Hillside was said to contain nearly a hundred teachers and pupils, most of them from Chicago. In 1933 the first Taliesin apprentices remodeled the building. The gymnasium became the theater, the chemistry rooms are now an exhibition space, and an extension to the north is now used as a drafting room. Along each side of this room were two rows of bedrooms for the apprentices. In the 1970s the roof and trusses were removed and rebuilt, opening the saw-tooth clerestories, during the early stages of the multi-million dollar restoration program now administered by the Taliesin Preservation Commission.

Right: The school building proper is on the right of this photograph.

1903

It was sometime this year that Frank Lloyd Wright began to design a single-story brick house with wood trim for Edwin H. Cheney and his wife, Mamah (pronounced Maymah).

Frank Lloyd Wright's home life and personal circumstances
In the autumn, Frank and Kitty's sixth and last child, Robert Llewellyn, always called Llewellyn in the family, was born.

1903 BUILDINGS CONTINUED

Larkin Company Administration Building, Buffalo, New York.

Abraham Lincoln Center, Chicago, Illinois. (*Above.*)

J. J. Walser House, Chicago, Illinois. (*Left.*)

PROJECTS

Chicago and Northwestern Railway: stations for Chicago suburbs, Chicago, Illinois.

Lamp House I, Madison, Wisconsin.

Roberts Quadruple Block Plan (24 houses), Oak Park, Illinois.

Waller House II, Charlevoix, Michigan.

Studio House, Oak Park, Illinois.

Larkin Company Administration Building

Buffalo, New York

Demolished: 1949–50

Wright got this job through his friendship with William E. Martin, from Oak Park, whose brother, Darwin D. Martin, worked with Larkin, the founder of the mail-order business named after him. This strikingly innovative structure was one of the finest buildings of Wright's early period, notable for its monolithic structure and large atrium. It not only represented a new architectural form but was also a radical concept of what an office should be. The architecture profession at the time, however, didn't realize the importance of the building and in a review of the building in the *Architectural Record* (April 1908), Russell Sturgis called it "wholly repellent as a work of human artisanship." The Larkin building used plate glass and air-condi-tioning, a first in commercial buildings, showing Wright's well-known commitment to the therapeutic value of space and light. The main workroom was a Roman-style atrium surround-ed by balconies that allowed light to stream into the central building space thus reducing the need for artificial illumination. The steel-framed building clad in brick, inside and out, was also designed to be fireproof. The use of plate glass, office furniture of metal (not wood), and fireproof, noiseless magnesite flooring was all employed to this end.

For the internal spatial distribution, Wright introduced a central court rising to the full six-and-a-half-story height of the building, with side gallery offices illuminated both from the cen-tral court and from the side windows between the brick piers. The stairs of the main building were separate from it—they were housed in semi-attached towers at the outer corners and elevators were placed near the entrance and reception area. The stair towers had a dual purpose. As well as providing a commu-nication network, they also housed the ducts which served as air

Below: All that remains of the building are fragments of the foundation walls.

inlets for the ventilation and air-conditioning system—a truly notable feature of the building. Wright's "air-conditioning" system, designed just months after Wills Carrier had invented true air-conditioning, initially cleaned and heated the air while providing limited humidity control.

The demolition of the Larkin Building represented a great loss to Wright's architectural heritage and today all that remains of the building are fragments of the foundation walls. According to his autobiography he "took some satisfaction in learning how difficult—and how expensive—the Larkin Building was to destroy!"

1904

The building permit to begin work on the Cheney House at 520 North East Avenue, in Oak Park was issued in June. Cheney shared Wright's enthusiasm for automobiles and his wife, Mamah, belonged to the Nineteenth Century Women's Club along with Catherine Wright. The two women were, according to a local newspaper, "much in each other's company." It is conceivable that the commission for the Cheney House was an outgrowth of Catherine's friendship with Mamah. One can only imagine Catherine's sense of betrayal when Frank later left her for Mamah in 1909.

Frank Lloyd Wright's home life and personal circumstances
Frank's father, William Cary Wright, died on June 6 at the age of seventy-nine. Frank didn't attend the funeral and he inherited nothing from his father.

1904 BUILDINGS

Edwin H. Cheney House, Oak Park, Illinois. (*Far left, left, and below.*)

Susan Lawrence Dana House, Springfield, Illinois.

Darwin D. Martin House and Conservatory, Buffalo, New York.

Baldwin House I, Kenilworth, Illinois.

Bank Building I, Dwight, Illinois.

Clarke House, Peoria, Illinois.

House in Highland Park, Illinois.

Scudder House, Desbarats, Ontario, Canada.

Ullman House, Oak Park, Illinois.

Larkin Company Workmen's Rowhouses, Buffalo, New York.

Left: Dana House

Right: Darwin D. Martin House

Susan Lawrence Dana House

301-327 East Lawrence Avenue, Springfield, Illinois

Open to the public with tours available.

This house was to be Wright's most extravagant commission to date and is the largest and finest example of the architect's Prairie Style to survive. The original request from Mrs. Dana was for the old family Victorian mansion to be remodeled and enlarged in an Italianate Style. However, over two years, as the design and building progressed, remnants of the old house gradually disappeared. The thirty-five-room mansion is a series of grand rooms: a two-story high dining room, a library, and an art gallery housed in a detached building linked by a pergola to the long arm of the T-shaped plan of the main house. The impressive entrance to the house, with its broad, low-modeled

Right: Sculpture designed by Frank Lloyd Wright and executed by Richard Bock.

Below left and right: Dana House exterior and interior.

gables flashed with copper, is via a flight of low steps through a pair of Romanesque archways and under a vaulted space filled with art glass depicting stylized native wild flowers. The buff-colored Roman bricks of the exterior are set off by a band of bronze luster tiles, while inside the oak furniture is combined with brown and russet fabrics.

As befitted an art collector, there is much glass and sculpture by Richard Bock. On the entrance landing, halfway between the basement and the first floor, stands a terra-cotta obelisk, designed by Wright and executed by Bock, called "Flower in the Crannied Wall," after a line in a poem by Lord Tennyson. Outside the house, behind a two-story wood and masonry screen, was the garden and a reflecting pool.

The Dana Lawrence House was bought and restored by Mr. and Mrs. Charles C. Thomas in 1944 and represents a magnificent integration of architecture, interiors, and furnishings. When the Thomas's bought the house there were around 450 pieces of art glass and 103 pieces of Wright-designed furniture intact.

The Charles C. Thomas Company occupied the building for thirty-six years, until 1981, when the State of Illinois purchased the structure, which had been designated a National Historic Landmark in 1976. The Illinois State Historic Preservation Agency opens the house, now the Dana-Thomas House Historic Site, for free tours. The public entry and balcony over it are the only places where visitors are allowed to see the building as Wright envisioned it.

Far left: Interiors of Dana House.

Left: The Lawrence Memorial Library (1905).

1905

Frank Lloyd Wright's home life and personal circumstances
Exhausted by the traumas of building the Larkin Company
administration headquarters, Wright had lost his appetite for
work and left for a three-month stay in Japan, a country whose
culture and traditions—particularly artworks—had been of considerable interest to him for some time. Accompanied by his wife
and two clients, with whom they had struck up a friendship, Mr.
and Mrs. Ward W. Willits, Wright took the opportunity to buy a
considerable quantity of Japanese art. He was especially attracted by woodblock prints and the work of ukiyo-e artists like
Hiroshige, Hokusai, Utamaro, Harunobu, Kiyonaga, and
Sharaku. He didn't stop there; he bought bronzes, kakemono
(Japanese hanging scrolls), ceramics, and textiles, as well as folding screens of the Monoyama and Edo periods. His interest in
Japanese art was kindled in the 1890s and several authorities
claim to see a connection between the Japanese temple that
Wright saw at the World's Columbian Exposition of 1893 and
some of his own
buildings. He
returned from Japan
invigorated and had
acquired a valuable
collection of
Oriental art. He
became a consider-
able expert on
Japanese works in
particular, especially
the prints that he
was so fond of.

1905 BUILDINGS

**Mary M. W. Adams House,
Highland Park, Illinois.**
(*Below.*)

**Hiram Baldwin House,
Kenilworth, Illinois.**
(*Right.*)

**Charles E. Brown House,
Evanston, Illinois.**

Above and left: Heath House.

*Opposite (above and below):
Charles Brown House.*

1905 BUILDINGS CONTINUED

E-Z Polish Factory, Chicago, Illinois. (*Right.*)

Mrs. Thomas H. Gale Cottages, Whitehall, Michigan.

W. A. Glasner House, Glencoe, Illinois.

Thomas P. Hardy House, Racine, Wisconsin.

W. R. Heath House, Buffalo, New York.

A. P. Johnson House, Lake Delavan, Wisconsin.

Darwin D. Martin Gardener's Cottage, Buffalo, New York.

Lawrence Memorial Library (interior),
   Springfield, Illinois.

Rookery Building entrance, lobbies, and
   balcony-court remodeling, Chicago, Illinois.
   (*Opposite.*)

Smith Bank, Dwight, Illinois. (*Left and below.*)

Yahara Boat Club, Madison, Wisconsin.

PROJECTS
Barnes House, McCook, Nebraska
"House on a Lake"
"Varnish Factory"
Concrete Apartment Building, Chicago, Illinois.
Moore House pergola and pavilion, Oak Park,
   Illinois.

W.A. Glasner House

850 Sheridan Road, Glencoe, Illinois

East library enlarged. Basement finished. Two-car garage
added, west porch enclosed. Greenhouse added.
Front of the house can be seen from the street.

It has been suggested that the design for this house came out
of a competition for a two-person dwelling without servants.
Wright seems to have won. Situated on the brow of a ravine,
this building features an organization of space similar to the
later Usonian designs, in that no separate room was planned for
dining. It is one of several innovative designs that incorporated
an octagonal pavilion with den-library and sewing room
attached to the living room and a corner of the bedroom. The
main entry leads directly to the living room without a reception
room and is diagonally opposite the kitchen. Other entries are at
the rear of the house.

The house features finely detailed art glass with multi-color
inserts and the rough-sawn finish on the wood is typical of the
many Prairie Houses, with their horizontal board-and-batten
exteriors. In many remodelings of Wright houses, smooth lumber was used in the mistaken notion that this original rough
wood was used for economy. In fact, the architect preferred it.
The house was renovated in 1926 and again in 1938 with a further, somewhat degrading, restoration in 1972–1973 when
storm windows were installed over the art glass.

*Left: Rough hewn timber was
specified by Wright for the board-
and-batten surfacing of this Prarie
House facade.*

1906

1906 BUILDINGS

P. A. Beachy House, Oak Park, Illinois. (*Below.*)

K. C. DeRhodes House, South Bend, Indiana.

Grace Fuller House, Glencoe, Illinois.

A. W. Gridley House, Batavia, Illinois. (*Right.*)

Edward R. Hills House, Oak Park, Illinois. (*Opposite: below.*)

1906 BUILDINGS CONTINUED

P. D. Hoyt House, Geneva,
Illinois. (*Right and below.*)

George Madison Millard
House, Highland Park,
Illinois. (*Far right.*)

Frederick Nicholas House,
Flossmoor, Illinois.
(*Opposite: below.*)

1906 BUILDINGS CONTINUED

W. H. Pettit Memorial Chapel, Belvidere, Illinois.

River Forest Tennis Club, Illinois. (*Left.*)

Unity Temple, Oak Park, Illinois.

PROJECTS

Bock Studio-House, Maywood, Illinois.

Devin House, Eliot, Maine.

Gerts House, Glencoe, Illinois.

Ludington House, Dwight, Illinois.

Shaw House, Montreal, Canada.

Stone House, Glencoe, Illinois.

Above: Nicholas House

Unity Temple

Lake Street at Kenilworth Avenue, Oak Park, Illinois

Restored, in several stages, beginning in 1969.
Church open daily to the public, guided tours available.

The temple was built to replace the original Gothic Revival
cnurch that was destroyed by fire in June 1905. The Unitarians
who still practice there built it. The Unitarians do not adopt the
conventional Christian symbolism of the cross or (in architecture)
the spire so this temple differs in imagery from the usual churches. The plan of the cube containing the auditorium is a Greek
cross inscribed in a square and the space inside it is filled with
different levels of seating. The balconies brace the walls while
the tall square box, which hides the pyramidal weather skylight

*Right: High windows help to keep
noise to a minimum.*

*Below: The exterior is constructed
from concrete and the walls left
undressed.*

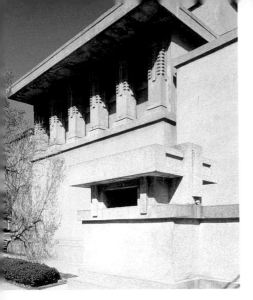

and the interior waffle grid that allows light through the ceiling, holds up the roof. Stairs to the upper level are contained in the pylons at the four corners. The high windows of the building help to keep the noise of the street and nearby railway lines to a minimum as well as providing ventilation. The building consists of two similar but unequal blocks —"Unity Temple" for worship and "Unity House" for social activities. The two blocks are joined by a low-entry hall link that contains the church office on a second level, which gives the building three activity areas. On the temple side no seat is more than 45 feet from the pulpit—"It remains a transcendent work bound to the earth and open to the heavens." (Quoted from Alice Sinkevitch's *AIA Guide to Chicago*.)

The exterior of the church is a monolithic mass of concrete and the walls, with their rough surface, were left undressed, exactly as they emerged from the wooden molds into which the concrete was poured. Original Wright plans specify a building in brick and stone, but the budget of $35,000 to build a church with an auditorium and a parish house for a congregation that

Above right: The interior is rich with art glass and fine wood trim.

numbered over 400 people, along with the potential offered by concrete, made the use of the medium irresistible. Wright found beauty in the concrete and made all the exterior walls and ornamentation from it. His use of poured concrete here is the first expression of the architect's fascination with a material he would explore and develop over the following fifty-five years.

Most buildings conceal their engineering but the Unity Temple has no qualms about exposing it. (The complete history of the engineering of this building has recently been fully researched by Joseph Siry in *Unity Temple*, Cambridge Press). In 1952, Wright stated, "Unity Temple is where you will find the first real expression of the idea that the space within the building is the reality of that building." Today, the building is still owned and occupied by the congregation that commissioned it, the Unitarian Universalist Church in Oak Park. The Unity Temple has been designated by the American Institute of Architects as one of the seventeen American buildings designed by Wright to be retained as an example of his architectural contribution to American culture. It not only marked a definite break with traditional ecclesiastical architecture but, with its exposed pebble surface, was a pioneer American building in reinforced concrete.

**Frank Lloyd Wright
writings & publications**

Hiroshige: An Exhibition of Color prints from the Collection of; The Art Institute of Chicago, 1906. The text of the accompanying catalog to the exhibition of prints was the first in a series Wright wrote concerning Japanese woodblock prints and the arts of Japan. Wright stated again and again that it was the simplicity of the prints, "the elimination of the insignificant" and their underlying geometry that first attracted him. These same principles were critical to his architectural philosophy, and he would often use the prints to illustrate his arguments.

Left and far left: Unity Chapel.

1907

1907 BUILDINGS

George Blossom Garage, Chicago, Illinois.

Cummings Real Estate Office, River Forest, Illinois.

George Fabyan House remodeling, Geneva, Illinois. (*Right and far right.*)

Fox River Country Club remodeling, Geneva, Illinois.

Stephen M. B. Hunt House, La Grange, Illinois.

McCormick House, Lake Forest, Illinois.

Pebbles & Balch Shop, Oak Park, Illinois.

Andrew T. Porter House, 'Tan-y-deri', Spring Green, Wisconsin. (*Far right, below*)

Harvey P. Sutton House, McCook, Nebraska.

F. F. Tomek House, Riverside, Illinois.

Burton J. Westcott House, Springfield, Ohio.

PROJECTS
McCormick House, Lake Forest, Illinois.
Municipal Art Gallery, Chicago, Illinois.
Porter House II, Spring Green, Wisconsin.

Frank Lloyd Wright writings & publications
"A Fireproof House for $5,000," Ladies' Home Journal, April 1907)
The Curtis Publishing Company commissioned the design for the Ladies' Home Journal in April. Here Wright proposed the use of poured concrete for residential design. Its particular advantage was to render the building fireproof.

Stephen Hunt House

345 South Seventh Avenue, LaGrange, Illinois

The house can be seen from the street.

The best built example of "A Fireproof House" (as advertised in the April 1907 edition of the *Ladies' Home Journal*), it is one of the most economical plans ever devised using the most basic architectural form—a cube. Each room of the house is made to look larger than its dimensions by the technique of visually borrowing space from the other rooms. It represents the maturation of Wright's thoughts on how best to arrange space in a square plan, or what might have been his American four-square house. In this house, the fireplace is moved from the outer wall to the center of the structure with the living room occupying half the main floor. The dining room continues from this space as an L. The kitchen occupies the other quarter and a small entry space is added onto the side opposite the dining room, with the stairs adjacent but within the house square. The dining room, which is larger than a quarter of the square, pushes the kitchen beyond the square and so violates the standard geometry of the designed fireproof house, but this allows for a larger second bedroom upstairs.

This house illustrates Wright's use of a basic tripartite spatial organization in his design. It places the living room—the area of main activity—in one space, separated from the entry, hallway, stairs, and from ancillary activity spaces, such as the kitchen, utilities, and sleeping quarters. This spatial idea, as a basic element of organic design, is to be found in Wright's Usonian dwellings as well as some of his non-residential structures.

Built in the heyday of the Prairie House, it is a square-plan, wood and plaster house, very economical to build even by

Above: The Hunt House was built in the heyday of Wright's Prarie Style designs.

today's standards. The original plan was a concrete construction, which would have made it fireproof. It is the windows of the Hunt House that makes it superior to other similar buildings. In the living room the glass extends up to the plane of the ceiling and there are slit lights at the ends of the four large front windows that allow the jambs to be free of the wall. Renovation has seen the terraces enclosed but the oak woodwork and the Tiffany brick fireplace have been fully restored.

1908

By 1908, Frank Lloyd Wright, with his Prairie House designs, had originated most of the principles that are today the fundamental concepts of modern architecture.

Wright's interest in Japanese cultural traditions led him to collaborate with Frederick Gookin, an authority on Japanese prints, to present a collection of Hiroshige prints at Chicago's Institute of Art. They became good friends and Gookin, an enthusiastic fan of all things Japanese, became convinced that Wright was the only man who could design and build the new Imperial Hotel in Tokyo and, therefore, determined to secure the job for his friend. The existing hotel was about to be pulled down and rebuilt, partly with the intention of attracting more American tourists. One of Gookin's many Japanese contacts was the manager of the Imperial, Aisaku Hayashi, and he eventually convinced him that Wright was the only man who could combine the spirit of Japanese architecture with American building techniques and standards.

Frank Lloyd Wright's home life and personal circumstances

Wright's so-called "prairie years" were coming to an end and he was growing restless and dissatisfied with life and work in his Oak Park home and studio. As the year drew to a close, he wrote to his client and patron Darwin D. Martin, "In my own life there is much that is complex, at least. Life is not the simple thing it should be if within myself I could find the harmony that you have found. It is difficult for me to square my life with myself, and I cannot rest until it is done or I am dead."

Kuno Francke, Professor of the History of German Culture at Harvard, went to Oak Park to see Wright's work at first hand. He suggested that Wright should visit Germany, which he did the following year.

1908 BUILDINGS

Edward E. Boynton,
  Rochester, New York.

Browne's Bookstore,
  Chicago, Illinois.

Avery Coonley House,
  Riverside, Illinois.

Alexander Davidson House,
  Buffalo, New York. (*Left.*)

Robert W. Evans House,
  Chicago, Illinois.

Eugene A. Gilmore House
  "Airplane House,"
  Madison, Wisconsin.
  (*Below left.*)

L. K. Horner House, Chicago,
  Illinois.

Horseshoe Inn, Estes Park,
  Colorado.

Horse Show Association
  Fountain, Oak Park, Illinois.

Meyer May House, Grand
  Rapids, Michigan
  (*Overleaf, top right*).

Ingwald Moe House, Gary,
  Indiana.

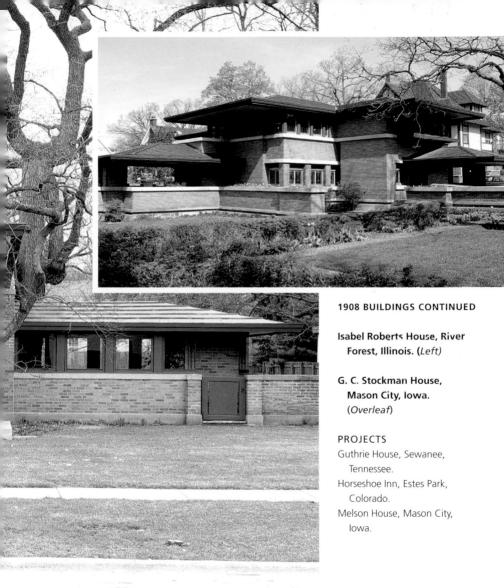

1908 BUILDINGS CONTINUED

Isabel Roberts House, River Forest, Illinois. (*Left*)

G. C. Stockman House, Mason City, Iowa. (*Overleaf*)

PROJECTS
Guthrie House, Sewanee, Tennessee.
Horseshoe Inn, Estes Park, Colorado.
Melson House, Mason City, Iowa.

Frank Lloyd Wright
writings & publications

In The Cause of Architecture, Architectural Record No. 3, March 1908.

This was Wright's first developed statement about the cause to which he devoted his life. It was accompanied by eighty-seven illustrations—photographs of executed buildings and drawings for other projects. With its circulation extending not only to the American professionals but to their European counterparts as well, this early publication began to disseminate the ideas of Frank Lloyd Wright to a substantial audience. When this article was published Wright was forty-one years old and at the top of his profession. He already realized his buildings would exert tremendous influence on modern architecture.

Avery Coonley House

281 Blooming Bank (living room), 300 Scottswood Road (bedroom wing), Riverside, Illinois

The dining-room side of the house can be seen from the street.

Coonley House is one of Wright's first works using the zoned plan and, according to his biography, he believed he put his best work into it. The house incorporates two of Wright's strongest beliefs—the centrifugal plan and the raised basement—and is one of the most outstanding examples of the Prairie House. The outer walls have a banded effect, their bronze-colored inlaid tiles are used to form a geometrical pattern on the upper half of the plaster-surfaced, wood-trimmed house, while the lower parts of the wall are coated in a creamy-colored fine sand plaster. Avery Coonley was a Christian Scientist and the design of the house was dictated by the tenets of this church that dictates

Below and right: The Coonley house exterior is plaster-surfaced with a wood trim.

Below right: Bronze-colored inlaid tiles form a geometrical pattern on the upper half of the wall.

its practitioners conduct interviews. Two stairways were constructed so the interviewees could not see each other when entering and leaving.

The house is built to a U-shaped plan and has raised living quarters in the Prairie Style, with a pavilion linking the various spaces. The living and dining rooms, together with the service areas, are located in the western half of the U while the bedrooms are located in the eastern half, all on the second level. All the main rooms, with the exception of the large, centrally located children's playroom, look out over lawns and the garden from a carefully calculated height. This puts into practice the architect's opinion that rooms dedicated to enjoyment should have a pleasing outlook. The Wright–designed interior fittings and furniture are in his preferred autumnal hues, enriched by the light which falls through the leaded casements and ceiling lights.

As part of the estate the gardener's cottage (290 Scotswood Road) was built in 1911 and the coach house, originally a stable, the same year. Both buildings were featured in the original published plans but were constructed later. The property was converted into three separate apartments in the 1950s and the coach house is now on a separate plot.

Above left: Most of the main rooms look out over lawns.

Left and far left: Exterior views of the Coonley House.

1909

Architects who were more conventional than Wright opposed his unorthodox methods and, beset with personal difficulties and professional antagonisms, he passed a year of self-imposed exile in Europe. He first went to Germany in 1909 at the invitation of the publisher Ernst Wasmuth who was to produce the portfolio *Ausgeführte Bauten und Entwürfe* (see 1910) that would become a collector's item.

It was while Wright was designing a typical Tuscan house in Fiesole, (1909–1910) near Florence, that his imagination seems to have been galvanized and brought to bear on the challenge of designing a house for him that would express everything he thought and believed in—the idea of Taliesin.

Frank Lloyd Wright's home life and personal circumstances

Wright had rashly fallen in love with Mamah Borthwick Cheney, the wife of one of his neighborhood clients. Unable to live together in such a conservative society, they decided to flee to Europe. Wright, being able to take up a timely offer from Ernst Wasmuth to publish a complete monograph of his architectural work to date, shut down his Oak Park studio that had thrived for sixteen years, and abandoned his wife and six children. Mamah Borthwick Cheney left her husband and two children to join him. At the same time, Wright uncharitably justified his actions by blaming his family for his financial problems, which actually had far more to do with his own extravagance than anything else. Such excuses did nothing to reduce the ensuing public scandal that seriously inhibited his career.

1909 BUILDINGS

Frank J. Baker House, Wilmette, Illinois. (*Right.*)

Bitter Root Inn, Darby, Montana.

City National Bank and Hotel, Mason City, Iowa.

William H. Copeland House, Oak Park, Illinois.

Laura Gale House (Mrs. Thomas Gale), Oak Park, Illinois.

J Kibben Ingalls House, River Forest, Illinois.

Frederick C. Robie House, Chicago, Illinois.

Scoville Park Fountain, Oak Park, Illinois.

Oscar Steffans House,
Chicago, Illinois.

George C. Stewart House,
Montecito, California.
(*Left and opposite.*)

Stohr Arcade, Chicago,
Illinois.

Thurber Art Gallery, Chicago,
Illinois.

Waller House: bathing pavilion, Charlevoix, Michigan.

PROJECTS

Brown House, Geneva, Illinois.
"City Dwelling with Glass
Front"
Larwell House, Muskegon,
Michigan.
Lexington Terrace (second
project), Chicago, Illinois.
Roberts House, River Forest,
Illinois.
Town Hall, Glencoe, Illinois.
Town of Bitter Root, Darby,
Montana.
Waller House: bathing pavilion,
Charlevoix, Michigan.
Waller Rental Houses (three-
house scheme).

Frederick C. Robie House

5757 Woodlawn Avenue, Chicago, Illinois

House can be seen from the street, tours available.

Designed in its entirety, the Robie House is enriched inside with furnishings, art glass, and lighting fixtures that demonstrate all the earlier design elements of the Prairie residences, fully integrated into one of the most imposing buildings of the twentieth century. The size and quality of this house, along with the Avery Coonley House (see 1908), place them in a class of their own. The Robie House, without a basement, was set on a concrete base with brick piers and steel beams providing the structural framework upon which the three tiers of the house rest. The most notable first impression of the house is the Prairie low-hipped roof with its wide projecting eaves—a twenty-foot wide cantilevered terrace. Without space for a natural garden, Wright introduced nature into the enormous planters and urns. At each level, doors and windows open out onto terraces, balconies, and porches, thus bringing the outside into the house and vice versa.

The physical spaces inside the building have the areas which demand privacy—guest bedrooms, kitchen, and servants' rooms—located in a parallel block at the rear of the main block. The living room, central staircase, and the dining room create a single unit, separated but not divided by the

chimney. The master bedrooms are contained in the smaller area of the third level of the house.

The sobriquet "Battleship" was no doubt applied because many an observer saw the three levels of the house as "decks" and the projecting terraces as "bows" of a ship. This house may also be the first in American architecture to incorporate a garage as an integral part of the building.

The Robie House once faced demolition but it was saved by a property company who later transferred the ownership to the University of Chicago. It is today a National Historic Landmark and one of the seventeen structures designed by Wright to have earned special recognition from the American Institute of Architects as representative of his contribution to American culture. The furniture and carpets have today been substituted with near copies of the originals, some of which are in the University of Chicago's Smart Museum. The original cantilever couch can be found in the Metropolitan Museum, New York.

Above: Charles C. Robie House interior with original furniture.

Left: Robie House exterior.

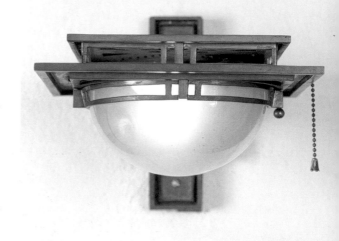

Above: The fireplace provides separation between the living and dining rooms.

Right: Lighting designed by Frank Lloyd Wright.

Opposite, above and below: Robie House interiors showing original furniture in situ.

1910

Ernst Wasmuth, a German publisher, published a complete monograph of Wright's architectural work to date. The publication of the two portfolios in 1910–1911 and the exhibition in 1911 in Berlin established Wright as an international architect whose qualities were increasingly being appreciated in Europe. His fame was much increased in architectural circles, influencing such key figures in contemporary architecture as Ludwig Mies van der Rohe and Le Corbusier. The complete folio of Wright's work to that date, a handsome edition known as the *Ausgeführte Bauten und Entwürfe* became a collector's item. Wright worked out a complex business arrangement with Wasmuth by which he would buy the American rights.

Frank Lloyd Wright's home life and personal circumstances

Far away from Chicago and personal reproach, Wright and Mamah Cheney settled down to live in Berlin; he to his drawing board and she to a teaching post. For winter they went to Florence to avoid the heavy snow falls, taking a house in Fiesole, near Florence, and decided to stay on there, captivated by the wonderful Tuscan villas and gardens. To help with the vast number of ink drawings required by the Wasmuth monograph, Wright sent for his son Lloyd and one of his draftsmen, Taylor Woolley.

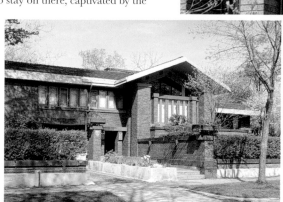

1910 BUILDINGS

J. H. Amberg House, Grand Rapids, Michigan. (*Left and inset.*)

Como Orchard Summer Colony (partly built), Darby, Montana.

Edward P. Irving House, Decatur, Illinois.

Jessie R. Ziegler House, Frankfort, Kentucky.

PROJECTS
House-Studio, Viale Verdi, Fiesole, Italy.

Frank Lloyd Wright writings & publications
Ausgeführte Bauten und Entwürfe, Berlin, 1910.
Wright's introductory text to the monograph opens with extraordinary lavish praise for the early Italian Renaissance (he refers to them as Gothic) architects, painters, and sculptors whom he especially admired. He considers his own work, which is of the twentieth century and on American soil: "I suggest that a revival, not of the Gothic style, but of the Gothic spirit, is needed in the Art and Architecture of the modern life of the world."

Edward P. Irving House

Decatur, Illinois

This was the last commission Wright undertook before setting sail to Europe, with Mamah Bordwick Cheney, to produce the Wasmuth Portfolio. The original plans reveal the architect working as he always intended, designing not only the house but also all its furniture and furnishings, down to the fabrics and rugs. Built-ins are found throughout the house and there are grills with art glass in both the upstairs ceiling and stairwell, each lit by skylights in the attic with added electric lighting for nighttime use.

The plan of the house shows a dining room and library flanking a twenty feet long living room. The extension is nearly doubled by porches to the east and west while interior volume is further doubled by a kitchen, servants' dining room, and reception hall. Two sleeping porches—to counter the humid

Right: Wright designed all the furnishings including the fabrics and rugs.

Below: The house is extended by porches to the east and west.

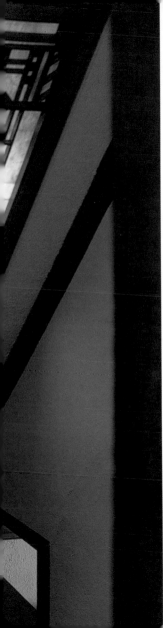

summers on the prairie, supplement the five bedrooms, four for the family and one for the maid. The main structure is capped by red tile and the separate garage design is of tan brick. Marion Mahony and Hermann von Holst, working out of Wright's Chicago office, moved the foundation thirty feet west of the original plan and changed the plaster to brick. It was Mahony who enclosed the second-level porch with glass and squared off the entry. Today, the kitchen and pantry have been converted into a single room, and the coatroom combined with the powder room.

The commission for the buildings came to Wright from the prominent businessman Edward P. Irving and construction ran from 1910 to 1913. Edward died in 1923 but his wife, Florence, remained in the house until 1950. Three owners followed until the house fell vacant in 1972 when Alice L. Sloan purchased it.

Left: Stairwell showing grill with
art glass designed by Wright.

1911

Wright rebuilt his life after the trauma of the 1909–1911 period. With his reputation assured on both sides of the Atlantic, he established Taliesin, the home and school he built for himself in Wisconsin. He established a studio-workshop for apprentices who assisted him on his projects and embarked on a career of ever-widening achievements. He began to reinforce the philosophical underpinnings of his innovative "organic" building style, with its bold claim that the structural principles found in natural forms should guide modern American architecture. Wright's view of architecture was essentially romantic.

1911 BUILDINGS

Herbert Angster House, Lake Bluff, Illinois.

Oscar B. Balch House, Oak Park, Illinois. (*Below.***)**

Walter Gerts House, Whitehall, Illinois.

Frank Lloyd Wright's home life and personal circumstances

By 1911, the Wasmuth monograph was finished so Wright and Mamah Borthwick Cheney decided to return to the United States. But where could they go? Chicago was impossible, so they decided on the old family domains of Spring Green, Wisconsin. Wright's mother helped out by giving him a tract of family land that she had earmarked for a cottage for herself. The land, although very hilly and rocky, was ideal for a rural estate and Wright christened it Taliesin, the Welsh for "shining brow." Wanting to make Mamah his legal wife, Wright pleaded with Catherine for a divorce, but, still hurt and angry, she refused.

Taliesin I

Route 23, Taliesin, Spring Green, Wisconsin

The building is open in the spring, summer, and part of the autumn with several tour options available at the Visitors' Center.

Taliesin is the major dedicated Wrightian complex in the United States and the epitome of his genius. None of Wright's other buildings serve such complex functions, and yet retain their graceful rusticity. "Geometry allowed the artist to seize upon the essentials and give to the image of a natural form that inner harmony which penetrates the outer form and is its determining character" (Neil Levine). This is the organic principle that is the basis for all Wright's work.

When Wright returned from Europe in 1911 with Mamah Borthwick Cheney, his mother gave him a tract of family land in Spring Green, Wisconsin, just off the Wisconsin River, in a valley opposite the "Welsh Hills" of Bryn Maur, Bryn Carol, and Bryn Bach. The land, although very hilly and rocky, was ideal for a rural estate and Wright christened it Taliesin, the Welsh for "shining brow." The name, originally used purely to indicate Wright's house, has come to identify the whole valley.

At Taliesin the architect was able to develop fully and display his ideas of using natural materials and elements combined in a setting of harmony and sympathy with the overall environment. Wright desired that Taliesin should be "of the hill, not on the hill." The Villa Medici in Tuscany, Italy, inspired his first house and he relished the challenge of designing a house that would express everything he thought and believed. The complex eventually incorporated a farm and other functional buildings stretching gradually across the hill. In the end Taliesin had acquired three thousand acres and it is possible that Wright's ambition was to buy up enough land to make it a state park. Taliesin has been designated by the American Institute of

Architects as one of the seventeen buildings designed by Wright
to be retained as an example of his architectural contribution to
American culture and is now preserved and run by the
Foundation. The Taliesin Preservation Commission oversees the
buildings that encompass the complex: Romeo and Juliet
Windmill (1896), Andrew Porter house (1907), and Taliesin (I
1911, II 1914, III 1925).

1912

The German monograph of Wright's work, *Ausgeführte Bauten und Entwürfe von Frank Lloyd Wright*, was published, making his works and name well known throughout Europe. Commissions were rolling in and he would have made a comfortable living were it not for his penchant for expensive clothes, stylish cars, extravagant living, and, of course, compulsive Japanese art collecting. "Take care of the luxuries," he said airily, "and the necessities will take care of themselves."

1912 BUILDINGS

Coonley Playhouse,
    Riverside, Illinois.

Lake Geneva Hotel,
    Wisconsin.

William B. Greene House,
    Aurora, Illinois. (*Left, far
    left and overleaf*)

Francis W. Little House
    "Northorne".
    Little House, library,
    Allentown, Penn.
    Little House, living room,
    New York City, New York.

Park Ridge Country Club,
    Park Ridge, Illinois.

PROJECTS

Dress Shop, Oak Park, Illinois.
Florida House, Palm Beach,
    Florida.
Kehl Dance Academy House and
    Shops, Madison, Wisconsin.
San Francisco Call newspaper
    building, San Francisco,
    California.
Schoolhouse, LaGrange, Illinois.
Taliesin Cottages (two buildings),
    Spring Green, Wisconsin.

Frank Lloyd Wright writings & publications

*The Japanese Print: An
    Interpretation* published as a
    book by Ralph Fletcher
    Seymour.
Wright's "interpretation" is real-
    ly an in-depth study not just
    of the print but of the entire
    culture that it reflects and
    records.

Left: William B. Greene House

Francis W. Little Residence II

Northome, Deephaven, Minnesota

Demolished 1972.
Living room reconstructed in the Metropolitan Museum of
   Art, New York City.
Library reconstructed in the Allentown Art Museum,
   Pennsylvania.
Bedroom wing stored at Domino's Farms, Ann Arbor,
   Michigan.

The house was designed during a difficult period in Wright's life
and, although the original designs were somewhat lackluster,
criticism by Little inspired the architect into producing a much
higher standard of work. Wright's first building in Minnesota,
the Little House, perched along a ridge overlooking Lake
Minnetonka and provides one of the best examples of his ability
to integrate the design of a building into its surrounding landscape. The fifty-five-foot living room, perhaps Wright's most
spacious domestic interior from his Prairie period, opened its
secondary view inland. Sleeping quarters were also on the main
and upper floors, opposite the living room and over the dining
space, which nestled in a hilly depression.

In the early 1970s, Little's daughter built a new house adjacent to the original building but the design was so close to the
original that the authorities insisted that one of the buildings
would have to go. Instead of relocating or demolishing the
newer house, sadly, she decided to demolish the original.
Fortunately, informed by nearby Wright clients the Loveness's, a
friend of theirs, Edgar Taefel, decided to seek the help of his
influential associates in New York.

One of Taefel's acquaintances was Arthur Rosenblatt, the
Director of the Metropolitan Museum of Art, and he decided to
have the whole original Little building, with the exception of the
library, dismantled and moved to New York. Taefel managed to

persuade the Allentown Museum in Pennsylvania to purchase the library, where it is installed as a permanent exhibit. Obvious-ly it would have been preferable if the Little House had never been demolished but a visit to the American wing of the Metropolitan Museum, and particularly to the Little exhibit, is the only way many people can experience being in a Wright–designed interior. The reconstructed living room is set in a depression like the original dining room and fortunately, even in this indoor setting, natural light prevails to give a real sense of the ambience of the original.

Windows from the Little Residence are in the collections of museums in Dallas, Minneapolis, and Karlsruhe.

1913

Frederick Gookin was an authority on Japanese prints and collaborated with Wright to present a collection of Hiroshige prints at Chicago's Institute of Art. They became good friends and Gookin, an enthusiastic fan of all things Japanese, became convinced that his friend was the only man who could design and build the new Imperial Hotel in Tokyo.

Wright returned (with Mamah) to Japan to press his case; staying for six months while he formulated preliminary plans for the Hotel. (The completed hotel was one of Wright's favorite buildings and he boasted about it all his life. He was to make frequent visits to Japan, a country he loved, and spent the bulk of his time there from 1919 to 1922.)

In 1913, Frank Lloyd Wright and Mamah Cheney published the translated writings of the Swedish feminist Ellen Key. These writings included "The Woman Movement" and her views on free love.

1913 BUILDINGS

**Harry S. Adams House II,
Oak Park, Illinois.** (*Right.*)

PROJECTS

Block of City Row Houses, Chicago, Illinois.

Carnegie Library, Ottawa, Ontario, Canada.

Hilly House, Brookfield, Illinois.

Kellog House, Milwaukee, Wisconsin.

Mendelson House, Albany, New York.

Frank Lloyd Wright's home life and personal circumstances
On Wright's voyage to Japan he spent considerable time and
money on Japanese works of art, particularly on the prints of
ukiyo-e artists Harunobu, Kiyonaga, Utamaro, Sharaku,
Hokusai, and Hiroshige. Japanese folding screens of the
Momoyama and Edo periods were also avidly sought by him,
along with kakemono, bronzes and ceramics, and textiles.

Harry S. Adams House

710 Augusta Blvd, Oak Park, Illinois

The main facade of the house can be seen from the street.

This is Wright's last work in Oak Park and is built to a longitudinal plan, seventy feet end to end, that runs through from porte-cochere through porch, living room, and hall to dining room. A step leads up from the porte-cochere to a soffit-shielded walkway that passes an office and the living room on the way to the entry. The entry hallway separates the living room from the dining room, kitchen, and breakfast porch (since enclosed). On the second story were four bedrooms, three bathrooms (two small ones now converted into one larger one), and a sewing room—now part of the master bedroom.

The horizontality is emphasized by limestone bands at the sills level of both stories and white oak is used for the trim. The building is notable for Wright's design of perforated copper lighting fixtures both overhead and attached to the moldings. The art glass in the front door is worthy of particular note. The base glass is the typical straw amber, with an iridescent spray fired onto it. Each small piece of glass, with colors ranging from gold to green, is set at a different angle within the metal frame, with the result that the light reflections sparkle as one moves past the door. The complete structure, with its thin leaded windows and furniture, represents a masterful summation of Wright's Prairie ideals just at the time he was looking forward to new ideas.

Left: The Adams House is Wright's last work in Oak Park.

1914

House Beautiful, an American journal founded to promote the ideals of the Arts and Crafts Movement, published the last Prairie House designs of Wright's in 1914.

By now a number of influential friends and admirers were calling for Wright to get the job to build the Imperial Hotel in Japan and he finally secured the commission. He was also commissioned by Edward C. Waller to design the Midway Gardens Pleasure Palace in Chicago. This and other jobs convinced Wright of the necessity of opening a Chicago office to be nearer the majority of his clients and contractors. Shocked and bereft after the Taliesin tragedy (see below), Wright nevertheless vowed to rebuild it and in the process all but bankrupted himself.

Frank Lloyd Wright's home life and personal circumstances

One Saturday, August 15, while Wright was working on the Midway Gardens, he was called home from his Chicago office, back to Taliesin. There a scene of devastation and tragedy set out before him. A house servant, Julian Carlton, went berserk and deliberately set fire to Wright's house and slaughtered Mamah Cheney, her children, and four others. Two Taliesin draftsmen, Brodelle and Fritz; foreman Brunker; Billy Weston; his son Ernest; and David Lindblom, the gardener, were all having lunch in the main dining room at Taliesin. Mamah Cheney and her children were sitting elsewhere when Carlton attacked them with an axe. He then set fire to the house and attacked the occupants as they tried to flee. Mamah Cheney; her children John and Martha; Emil Brodelle; and Thomas Brunker were killed at the scene. Ernest Weston and David Lindblom died later from burns. Of the nine who had sat down to lunch that Saturday, only two, Herbert Fritz and Billy Weston, survived.

Carlton was found alive although he had attempted to commit suicide by swallowing hydrochloric acid. He was arrested and taken to prison where he died of starvation—because his throat was so badly burned by the acid—giving no explanation for his murderous attack.

1914 BUILDINGS

Midway Gardens, Chicago, Illinois.

Mori Oriental Art Studio, Chicago, Illinois.

**Taliesin II, Spring Green, Wisconsin
(destroyed by fire 1925).**

Women's Building, Spring Green, Wisconsin.

PROJECTS
Concert Gardens, Chicago, Illinois.
State Bank, Spring Green, Wisconsin.
United States Embassy building, Tokyo, Japan.
Vogelsang Dinner Gardens, Chicago, Illinois.

Frank Lloyd Wright writings & publications
In The Cause of Architecture: Second Paper, published in *The Architectural Record* (May)
—"Style, therefore will be the man, it is his. Let
his forms alone."

Midway Gardens

Southwest corner of Cottage Grove Avenue and 60th Street, Chicago, Illinois

Demolished: 1929

Conceived by Edward C. Waller Jr. this huge restaurant-cum-entertainment complex occupied an entire city block and appeared to have been something between a pleasure park and an open-air beer garden. It was notable for its patterned concrete blocks and brickwork and the whole complex seems to have been used by Wright for a rich and bold experiment in form and decoration, much of it inspired by Mayan sources and including abstract and Cubist compositions in the form of murals. The Midway Gardens revealed an entirely different approach to architecture and a new avenue into design. Wright created all the interior design elements, including sculpture, mural paintings, furniture, tableware, chinaware, and carpets.

The Summer Garden, a courtyard open to the elements, was a dancing and eating area with low arcades along the sides. The Winter Garden opposite, enclosed for year-round activity, was four floors high with a covered area roughly equal to the Summer Garden. The first floor was surrounded by a series of three terraces and was capped by a roof garden. Sculptures by Alfonso Lanelli adorned the work and the architect's son, John Lloyd Wright, assisted the construction supervision.

Among many of the unfortunate consequences of Prohibition in America was the destruction of the Midway Gardens less than ten years after its opening, when it was sold to a Chicago brewing company (the Edelweiss Brewing Company), which was put out of business by Prohibition.

1915

During this year Wright entered a period of exploration in his architecture where he expanded the simple square units of his first Prairie Houses and developed rectangles, triangles, and other geometric possibilities. He developed his architectural art for the average American more than for establishment leaders. The American Ready-Cut System of prefabricated houses and apartments reveal this tendency. What was missing was a system of construction that would meet this new democratic ideal. He was to find a solution in the early twenties with concrete.

1915 BUILDINGS

Emil Bach House, Chicago, Illinois. (*Left.*)

Sherman Booth House, Glencoe, Illinois. (*Far left and below.*)

Edmund F. Brigham House, Glencoe, Illinois.

Frank Lloyd Wright's home life and personal circumstances

After the Taliesin murders of 1914, Miriam Noel, whom Wright had never met, expressed such empathy that he agreed to her request to meet him. So started a self-destructive relationship that lasted the better part of ten years. Miriam was artistic but unbalanced, her emotional state aggravated by her addictions. She was also weak and depressed, emotions that Wright felt attracted by, but such raw feelings rapidly took away from their relationship. Nellie Breen, the housekeeper Wright had unwisely put in charge of Taliesin in 1915, objected to Miriam Noel's arrival at Taliesin. Her highly developed sense of propriety was offended and she protested as Wright's children were also in the house. After being dismissed by Wright, Nellie Breen accused him of violating the Mann Act—a statute that prohibited the transportation of women across state lines for "immoral purposes"—and demanded that Miriam Noel be deported. Wright's lawyer brought countercharges that Miriam had been threatened with bodily harm and the deportation orders were dropped with no formal charges brought against Wright under the Mann Act.

A.D. German Warehouse,
   Richland Center, Wisconsin.

Imperial Hotel, Tokyo, Japan.
   (*Left.*)
   Meiji Mura Museum,
   Imperial Hotel, Japan.

Ravine Bluffs Housing
   Development, Glencoe,
   Illinois.
   Lot 10: Charles R. Perry
   Lot 15: C. J. Ellis
   Lot 16: Frank B. Finch
   Lot 16: William W. Ross
   Lot 17: J. M. Compton
   Lot 22: S. J. Gilfillan
   Lot 22: Hollis R. Root

Wilbur Wynant House, Gary,
   Indiana.

PROJECTS
Chinese Restaurant, Milwaukee,
   Wisconsin.
Model Quarter Section
   Development, Chicago,
   Illinois.
Wood House, Decateur, Illinois.

Above left and far left: Ravine Bluffs Housing Development.

Left: Hollis R. Root House (Lot 22, Ravine Bluffs Housing Development.)

Albert D. German Warehouse

300 South Church Street, Richland Center, Wisconsin

Reduced visibility from the street, but tours available June–October.

After Wright moved from Chicago to Spring Green, he did most of his shopping at A.D. German, a dealer in coal, hay grain, and cement, and when it transpired Wright couldn't pay his bills, German took payment in the form of a design for a new warehouse. The new building was to be a place for storing and selling wholesale goods, as well as providing for tearooms, retail shops, and an art gallery. The design was a magnificent rectangular cube constructed from brick and cast-in-place concrete, evocative of ancient Mexican architecture. River sand helped the Chicago AA cement become the much-prized tan-colored concrete, much admired for its cleanliness, and the top story was encircled by finely patterned frieze in contrasting gray concrete. The reinforced concrete structure is designed with a grid of massive concrete columns strengthened with steel and with flaring capitals that carry the weight of the floor and the roof. The double brick-wall skin of the building created a cold storage without the need of mechanical refrigeration.

Progress was slow on the construction and the original projected cost of $30,000 was soon passed. The cost soon reached $125,000 and, as German's finances suffered during the war without a great deal of improvement afterward, construction stopped in 1921. Unpaid taxes cost German the building in 1932 and, though he bought it back in 1935, he finally lost it in 1937. After a succession of owners John H. Howe was hired as renovation architect and the building is, today, on the National Register of Historic Places. This is Wright's only work in the town of his birth and the building now houses the Richland Museum.

The first Imperial Hotel, Tokyo, Japan, was built in 1890. By the middle of the next decade, following the end of the Russo-Japanese War, foreign visitors to Japan had greatly increased and the demand for rooms could not be met. By 1909 a clear directive to build a new Imperial Hotel capable of meeting increased demand had been issued. A number of years passed, however, before an architect was hired. Wright appears to have secured the commission by 1913, but was not officially hired until 1916.

Frank Lloyd Wright's home life and personal circumstances
In December 1916 Frank and Miriam Noel sailed for Tokyo together where they lived while the architect worked on the Imperial Hotel project.

1916 BUILDINGS

American Systems Buildings:
Richards, Duplex Apartments, Milwaukee, Wisconsin.
Richards, Small House, Milwaukee, Wisconsin.

American Systems Bungalow (*Below left.*)**:**
Stephen Hunt, Oshkosh, Wisconsin.
J. J. O'Connor, Wilmette, Illinois.
William J. Vanderkloot, Lake Bluff, Illinois.

American Systems Two-Story House:
Burhans-Ellinwood & Co., Chicago, Illinois.
Hanney & Son, Evanston, Illinois.
Howard H. Hyde, Chicago, Illinois.
Delbert W. Meier, Monona, Iowa.

Joseph J. Bagley House, Grand Beach, Michigan.

Frederick C. Bogk House, Milwaukee, Wisconsin. (*Below.*)

W. S. Carr House, Grand Beach, Michigan.

Munkwitz Duplex, Milwaukee, Wisconsin.

Ernest Vosburgh House, Grand Beach, Michigan.

PROJECTS
Behn House, Grand Beach, Michigan.
Converse House, Palisades Park, Michigan.

Frank Lloyd Wright writings & publications
Plan by Frank Lloyd Wright published in *City Residential Land Development* (May).
The publication of this article, with its accompanying drawings, put on record Wright's first serious promotion of decentralization. The relief of urban and suburban congestion by means of more spacious, park-like planning was something that occupied him throughout his life.

Arthur L. Richards Duplex Apartments

2720-2734 West Burnham Street, Milwaukee, Wisconsin

The units are in various states of repair, with some fully restored.

In 1904, Arthur L. Richards was constructing houses and claiming that by building forty at a time he could make great savings over the individual buying a house part by part. This was an idea that Wright could readily accept a decade or so later.

These four separate buildings that make up the Burnham Street Duplex Apartments are all from American System ready-cut prefab plans of 1911 They each had upper and lower apartments and were originally of plaster surface and wood trim. Three of the buildings are identical in plan, while the fourth, that stands on a corner lot, employs a mirror-image plan.

Below and right: Three of the apartments are identical in plan, while the fourth (below) employs a mirror image plan.

Supervision of the Burnham Street project was by Russell Barr Williamson, Wright's chief drafting room assistant after the 1914 Taliesin fire. The first unit has been restored, the second given protective vinyl siding, and work on the third was completed in 1988. In 1990, the Milwaukee Common Council approved the creation of an historic district for these duplexes, the small Richards house—just east of the apartments and the Richards bungalow—has been re-sided.

Arthur L. Richards Small House

2714 West Burnham Street, Milwaukee, Wisconsin

Terrace enclosed.

This single-story flat-roofed house is from American System ready-cut prefab plans of 1911.

The entry to the building is concealed on the side, opening behind the fireplace that faces into the dual-purpose living and dining room. The kitchen is to the rear with two bedrooms and bath off to the side while the basement contains spaces for the laundry, heater, and coal supply. The bungalow employs an early mechanical form of air-conditioning by means of a kitchen vent and further vents in the chimney receiving air from soffit openings. The chimney also has a spout to drain the water, as the building has no eaves.

Many designs were drawn for the American System-Built group of projects, ranging from very small flat-roofed houses, such as this, through larger bungalows to three-story designs. Some of the larger designs featured hanging-garden terraces both in single-family and multi-family units. For every design, however, small or large, the parts were to be cut and shipped from Richards's Milwaukee factory to the site, where they would be assembled by local labor.

Below: This house is constructed from American System Ready-cut prefab plans of 1911.

Left: The house is kept cool by an early form of air-conditioning.

1917

To supplement his income further, and as a logical corollary of his own interest, Wright bought Japanese art for other American collectors—most notably for Mr. and Mrs. William Spalding of Boston, his close friend Frederick Gookin at the Art Institute of Chicago, Howard Masefield of the Metropolitan Museum of Art in New York City, and Sally Casey Thayer whose collection eventually went to the Spencer Museum at the University of Kansas. An exhibition of Wright's impressive collection of Japanese fine art, sponsored by the Arts Club of Chicago, ran from November 12 to December 5.

Frank Lloyd Wright's home life and personal circumstances

By now, Miriam Noel was a social recluse, but given to violent outbursts, many of them rooted in her constant insecurity. Yet, despite their ragng rows, somehow Wright and Miriam managed to stay together. With the money he was earning from the Imperial, Wright bought yet more Japanese art, but also forged ahead with the new Taliesin.

1917 BUILDINGS

**Henry J. Allen House,
Wichita, Kansas.** (*Left.*)

**Hayashi House, Tokyo,
Japan.**

**Odawara Hotel, Nagoya,
Japan.**

PROJECTS
Odawara Hotel, Nagoya, Japan.
Powell House, Wichita, Kansas.

Frank Lloyd Wright writings & publications
*Antique Color Prints from the
Collection of Frank Lloyd
Wright,* published as a cata-
logue by The Arts Club of
Chicago, Exhibition, 1917.

Henry J. Allen House

255 North Roosevelt Boulevard, Wichita, Kansas

Open to the public. Guided tours are available by appointment.

This is Wright's only private house in Kansas—but what a house. Built for presidential hopeful Henry Allen, governor of Kansas 1919–1923, the exterior appearance of a square, brick Prairie House hides the enclosed garden, terrace, pool, and summerhouse. The house encloses two sides with its L plan, a two-story east-west section and a single story north-south living room. The kitchen and servant's quarters, and a two-car garage are beneath the bedrooms and sleeping porch, which drop off a long tunnel gallery. In the living room, quarter-sawn oak provides the flooring and a cover board is used between wall and baseboard. Red gum is the millwork on both floors, with cypress employed solely as window sash. The interiors are exceptionally rich with gold leaf applied to the horizontal pointing of the masonry walls and an array of art glass installed in the bookcases. Mulberry paper in the ceiling lights has a Japanese maple-leaf stencil applied.

An elevator replaced the rear stairs after Mrs. Allen became an invalid and the house and gardens were completely renovated for A. W. Kincade in 1971–1972. Kincade bequeathed the house to Wichita State University in the 1980s; it was subsequently sold to the Allen-Lambe House Association that has fully restored the building.

Above: Wright's interior designs for the Allen House are rich with gold leaf applied to horizontal pointing.

Right: Art glass is installed in the furniture.

Left: An Oriental flavor is added with this screen.

Frank Lloyd Wright didn't desert the United States completely during the time he was supervising the building of the Imperial Hotel. He made frequent trips to the Midwest and, more particularly, to California. Back in 1914 he had met Aline Barnsdall, heiress to a Pennsylvania oil fortune. She was a keen thespian, whose dream was to build a theatrical complex, complete with homes and shops. She was a temperamental woman, prone to extreme mood swings, constantly changing her mind about what she wanted, and completely paranoid about being taken advantage of for her money.

This was also the year that Louis Sullivan telephoned Wright in Wisconsin and set the stage for their reconciliation after a twenty-five year schism.

Frank Lloyd Wright writings & publications

Chicago Culture; a speech, published in *On Architecture*.

The love-hate relationship that flourished between Wright and Chicago is evident in this article that was read to the Women's Aid Organization. Although it is a scathing criticism of the cheapness of the "nouveau riche" of the city, it also praises the many fine people Chicago produced. Wright extends special praise to his former employers Louis Sullivan and Dankmar Adler and at the same time praises other Chicago architects.

1918 BUILDINGS

Fukuhara House, Hakone, Japan.

Yamamura House, Ashiya, Japan.

PROJECTS

Count Immu House, Tokyo, Japan.
Viscount Inouge House, Tokyo, Japan.
Motion picture theater, Tokyo, Japan.

1919 PROJECTS

Japanese Print Gallery for the Spaulding Collection, Boston, Massachusetts.

"Monolith Homes," Racine, Wisconsin.

Tazaemon Yamamura Residence

Ashiya, Japan

This house, perched on a promontory above the left bank of the Ashiyagwa River, was originally constructed for the sake brewer Tazaemon Yamamura. It is constructed primarily from Oya stone, plaster, and Philippine mahogany (Lauan). The outlook faces south over the Osaka Bay and, as with many of Wright's designs, it is "at one" with its physical environs. Four stories lift the building up the hillside, and one 120-degree bend takes it round its eastern slope. The entry with the carport is at the lowest level, while at the top stands a roof terrace outside a dining room featuring a dramatic high-peaked ceiling. The third floor is the largest, containing two galleries spanning the length of the eastern exposure, with bedrooms and other activity spaces to the west and both sides of the 120-degree juncture.

The building has, in recent years, served as a company dormitory for the Yodagawa Steel Company (Yodagawa Seiko) of Osaka.

1920

During the twenties Wright invented a construction system of
concrete blocks fully suited to his newly developed Usonian
architecture. He developed this system with his eldest son Lloyd.
By 1921 his Usonian principle was fully developed and,
although he stated in 1952 that Alice Millard's House "La
Miniatura" in Pasadena, California, (1923) was his first Usonian
home, it wasn't until 1935 that the first homes he specifically
called Usonian appeared.

Frank Lloyd Wright's home life and personal circumstances
Despite all the ensuing problems and the abandonment of the
bulk of the project, Wright would complete one of his best-
known works, the Hollyhock House, and two other houses for
Aline Barnsdall. He maintained that in his entire career no
other client had caused him so much trouble or given him so
much grief, but the problems were worth overcoming.

1920 BUILDINGS

Aline Barnsdall "Hollyhock" House, Los Angeles, California. (*Left.*)
Kindergarten, Little Dipper.
Studio Residence A.
Studio Residence B, site.

PROJECTS
"Cantilevered Steel Skyscraper"
Apartments, theater, and
shops, Olive Hills, Los
Angeles.

Aline Barnsdall "Hollyhock" House

4808 Hollywood Boulevard, Los Angeles

Tours available.

Aline Barnsdall, an heiress to millions and a self-proclaimed "new woman," was convinced that she could change the world—albeit to her own beliefs.

This residence is a lavish construction of exposed concrete block on a very large scale and appears at first sight to be a monolithic concrete building. In fact it is constructed of hollow clay tiles, covered with stucco. Situated near the top of the 36-acre Olive Hill site, it is generously designed with a main block around a central courtyard, embellished with repeated motifs in finial form of abstract hollyhock designs (hence the nickname). The stylized hollyhock motif is repeated on stucco pinnacles on the exterior, the art-glass windows, and in the carved backs of the dining-room chairs. The house has the effect of an ancient temple and is richly ornamented with cast concrete forms, which Wright referred to as art stone. Their tawny gold color, which came from crushed, decomposed granite at the site, provided delightful contrast to the "silver-green" of the house.

Below, left, and overleaf: The Barnsdall house is reminiscent of a Mayan temple.

The entrance loggia, living room, music room, and library are organized in a T-shape, a device that Wright had employed in many of his early Prairie Houses. The house is centered on the west-facing

living room that leads out into an enclosed garden court that terminates in what was originally a circular reflecting pool, and is extended to long garden walls, terraces, and wings. The extended wings house the bedrooms and nursery in one; dining room, kitchen, and servants' rooms in the other. The building reflects the client's request for a half house, half garden, and incorporates numerous terraces, colonnades, and pergolas that link the interior spaces with the exterior spaces of the gardens. As in Wright's earlier designs, the living room is dominated by the central fireplace with a decorative overmantel and projecting hearth surrounded by a pool of water.

The building illustrates Wright's long-term interest in primitive, non-European forms—particularly pre-Columbian architecture. Recalling the Mayan nunnery replica he had seen in 1893, the poured concrete structure of the Hollyhock House was restored between 1974 and 1976 under the direction of Lloyd Wright. It has since been designated by the American Institute of Architects as one of seventeen buildings designed by

Above right: Living room and original furniture designed by Wright.

Right: Dining area and original furniture with hollyhock motif.

Left: The stone hearth is surrounded by a pool of water.

Wright to be retained as an example of his architectural contribution to American culture and is undoubtedly one of his great masterpieces. The original landscaping of Olive Hill was designed by Lloyd Wright but has long since been altered beyond recognition and has been a public park since 1927, when owner Aline Barnsdall gave it to the City of Los Angeles.

Left and above: Fine examples of Wright's art-glass designs.

Far left: The "hollyhock" motif also appears in the carpet designed by Wright.

1921

1921 BUILDINGS

Jiyu Gakuen, School of the Free Spirit, Tokyo, Japan.

PROJECTS

Doheney Ranch Development, near Los Angeles, California.
"Glass and Copper Skyscraper"
Baron Goto House, Tokyo, Japan.
Block House, Los Angeles, California.

Jiyu Gakuen School of the Free Spirit

Tokyo, Japan

Dining room expanded, and classroom wings added.

Jiyu Gakuen is widely known in English as the School of the Free Spirit. The whole building is drawn to a four-foot square unit module and the central area plan consists of two rectangles, with a second-story, forty-two-foot-long dining room at the rear, and a two-story high, thirty-two-foot-wide living room and classroom at the front. On the side of the main building, pairs of twenty-eight, thirty-two-foot rooms are connected by the protective roof creating breezeways. In line with Wright's principles regarding nature and architecture these breezeways bring the students close to nature even in a crowded urban environment.

Classrooms forming a U-shaped plan were added later to the original structure yet are perfectly integrated. The dining room has also been expanded by enclosing the sixteen-foot-square, flat-roofed spaces above the main-floor lavatories, and by a similar addition to the rear through former windows over flowerboxes. It is likely that all these additions are the work of Arata Endo, who supervised Wright's work in Japan and whose son continues his father's practice of organic architecture following his Taliesin apprenticeship.

1922

Frank and Miriam Noel returned full time to the United States when the Imperial Hotel was six months away from completion. The project had been all encompassing; Wright had designed every aspect of the building down to the carpets and door handles.

Frank Lloyd Wright's home life and personal circumstances

When Wright returned full time to the United States in 1922 his first wife, Catherine, at last agreed to grant him a divorce on the grounds of twelve years desertion. Wright hoped that by marrying Miriam he would be able to give her the emotional security she so badly needed and this would improve their relationship. Miriam was artistic but unbalanced, her emotional state aggravated by a morphine addiction. After six intolerable months Frank and Miriam separated.

Wright returned to Taliesin alone where he threw himself into working on a variety of ideas in company with a number of new assistants, many of these eager young architects from Europe. There were, however, no new major contracts coming in.

Frank Lloyd Wright writings & publications

The New Imperial Hotel, published in *Kaguku Chisiki* (April).
This was Wright's first published article about the hotel and was intended for a Japanese audience and any interested foreigners. It is a defense of his design and a critique of the contemporary Japanese architectural vision, or lack thereof. When asked why he didn't make the hotel more "modern," he replied, "There was a tradition there worthy of respect, and I felt it my duty as well as my privilege to make a building belong to them as far as I might."

1922 BUILDINGS

Lake Tahoe, Summer Colony.

Frank Lloyd Wright Studio, Los Angeles, California.

PROJECTS
Johnson Desert Compound and
   Shrine, Death Valley, California.
Merchandising Building, Los Angeles, California.
Desert Springs House, Mojave Desert, California.
Tahoe Summer Colony, Lake Tahoe, California.

1923

In 1923, the Kanto earthquake in Japan leveled everything else around it but left the Wright designed Imperial Hotel standing. Wright saw this as his ultimate triumph—to produce an earthquake-proof design, he had devised an elaborate foundation that allowed the hotel to survive.

Throughout the 1920s, Wright's work was mainly concentrated in California where the majority of his projects were private residences. Many of these buildings were romantic and almost illusory, reflecting his feelings about living in close harmony with nature and the land, and using the decorative stonework of pre-Columbian architecture. Wright's use of Mayan-inspired cast concrete dominated and culminated in what might be termed his fourth phase—the textile-block houses in the Los Angeles area of California. The Californian textile-block houses, like the majority of their Prairie predecessors, were multilevel structures. But the organization of activities in them was not as simplified and compact as it was in the single-story Usonians that were produced from 1935 on.

Frank Lloyd Wright's home life and personal circumstances

Wright became convinced that California, particularly southern California, was the place for his future. Its pre-European past gave the landscape an intangible romance and the fact that much of the state was desert appealed to him. He liked the vastness, the room to spread, and the idea that the land could be literally transformed by the introduction of water—this was nature in the raw, but it could be made accessible. At the prompting of his sister, Catherine, Wright moved his offices to the West Coast in the spring of 1923. His studio was temporarily located at Olive Hill, the complex he had designed for Aline Barnsdall in Hollywood.

1923 BUILDINGS

Samuel Freeman House, Los Angeles, California. (*Left.*)

Alice Millard House "La Miniatura," Pasadena, California.

John Storer House, Los Angeles, California.

PROJECTS
Martin House, Buffalo, New York.

Frank Lloyd Wright writings & publications
Experimenting with Human Lives, published by the Ralph Fletcher Seymour Co.
The Kanto earthquake disaster prompted Wright to make his observations on building construction in earthquake-prone areas. His own theories of construction, as evidenced in the Imperial Hotel, had been put to the ultimate test during the earthquake—the structure's survival had proved Wright correct.

The New Imperial Hotel, Tokio, published in *The Western Architect* (April).
Between April 1923 and February 1924 *The Western Architect* published three articles in which Wright explained his designs for the new Imperial Hotel. Wright pointed out that it was not an "office building hotel" along American lines, but "a system of gardens and sunken gardens and terraced gardens—of balconies that are gardens and loggias that are also gardens—and roofs that are gardens—until the whole arrangement becomes an interpenetration of gardens. Japan is Garden-land."

The second article, published in November, was the first of a two-part essay entitled *In The Wake of the Quake*. These articles were in reference to the disastrous Kanto earthquake but are not about the description of the tragedy, but rather about methods of construction that rendered the building capable of riding through the worst earthquake in Japan's recorded history.

Samuel Freeman House

1962 Glencoe Way, Hollywood, California

Open to the public. Tours available.

The Freeman House was the last and smallest, and arguably the most adventurous, of the Californian textile-block houses. It was built in a small and steeply sloping plot in the foothills of the Hollywood Hills. The major feature of this house was the view overlooking Hollywood in its entirety.

In response to his client's wishes and because of the cramped space the site afforded, Wright designed a concrete block dwelling that was light and airy in a manner not usually associated with concrete. As the house was turned away from the street, the front elevation is essentially a blank wall, while the back is almost entirely glazed. The house incorporates the open plan and the central hearth of the earlier Prairie House. It is on two levels, with the living room, kitchen, balcony, and garage on the entry level, and sleeping quarters and terrace one story below.

The construction materials consisted of fir-painted red-wood, eucalyptus for appearance, and plain and patterned textile block. There are both left-hand and right-hand versions of the square and

Right: The back of the house is almost entirely glazed offering superb views of the streets below.

Below: Detail of Wright's textile-block design.

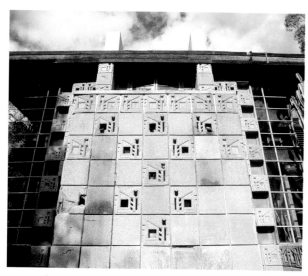

chevron asymmetrically-patterned blocks, and sometimes inverted. The building exploits the ornamental potential of concrete blocks combined with traces of Mayan, Mogul, Japanese, and European modernism.

Supervision of the construction and landscaping were by Lloyd Wright who also did the working drawings. The Freemans lived in their home for more than fifty years but upon Mrs. Freeman's death in 1986 ownership of the house passed to the University of Southern California via a living trust.

Above: Entrance portico to Freeman Residence.

Left: Sleeping area with compact furniture design by Wright.

Far left: Living room with original furniture designed by Wright.

Alice Millard House, "La Miniatura"

645 Prospect Crescent, Pasadena, California

This, arguably the finest of its kind, was the first example of the four textile-block houses constructed in the Los Angeles area. Thirty years later Wright was to refer to this house as his first Usonian House. It was constructed by stacking concrete blocks, three inches thick, adjacent to and on top of each other without visible mortar joints. The blocks in the Millard House have no reinforcing metal rods but are laid with expanded metal on a conventional mortar bed.

Flying in the face of wisdom, the house was built in the bottom of an arroyo—a kind of ravine —which are dry for most of the year but in rainy seasons carry a vast amount of water. Partly because the narrowness of the arroyo precluded the ground-hugging horizontality of the Prairie House style and partly because of Wright's textile-block system, the Millard House is a box. Visitors enter the house through a paved court leading to an entrance covered by a low bridge that spans from the house to a roof terrace over the attached garage. The two-story-high living room is delicately lit by a high window wall, composed of glass doors at the lower level, and a pattern of pierced concrete blocks set with glass above.

The decision to build the house in the bottom of the arroyo turned out to be a mistake. The culvert, that for over fifty years had taken the street water away below the basement level, overflowed and rose to the level of the dining room, burying the floors under layers of mud. The house was subsequently cleaned up with the assistance of the Pasadena City authorities. Today in its overgrown gardens the effect of intimacy and nature makes it seem like a half-excavated Central American monument.

Above and right: Gated entrance to studio and expansive studio interior.

Top: Detail of textile-block design.

John Storer House

8161 Hollywood Boulevard, Hollywood, California

This, the second of the four Los Angeles textile-block houses, is a most lavish example of the genre. The house looks southward toward Hollywood and Los Angeles while the northern view looks into a courtyard carved out of the ascending hillside and is designed to a split-level plan with wings to each side—bedrooms to the west, service to the east. The head of its T–plan is three levels, capped by an open terrace set at half-level to the main-floor dining room and two-story living room below.

Parallel rows of hollow concrete-block paired piers, on the end elevations, support wooden beams and joists in the central volume of the building. Unlike the blocks in the Millard House, the Storer House blocks were to be formed under pressure in machine-made metal molds, then removed from the molds and allowed to dry over a period of ten days. The building employed

Below: The house looks south-ward toward Hollywood and L.A.

Right and below right: Wright, as usual, designed all the furniture and fittings.

four different block patterns and is the only house in which Wright used more than one design. There is a dominant pattern, however: the corner blocks are decorated with a concave pattern of concentric half squares that read as a whole square when the two faces of the blocks are seen.

In this house, Wright, as usual, designed all the furniture and fittings, and the character of the exterior decorative forms can be seen in the view of the living room. Lloyd Wright supervised construction and Wright's great-grandson, Eric Wright, was the architect for the restoration of the building in the 1980s.

1924

By 1924 Wright was back at Taliesin, separated from Miriam Noel, and at work on new commissions. The new building that Albert M. Johnson commissioned him to design for the National Life Insurance Company was to be a copper and glass tower. If it had been built, it would have been a Chicago landmark and put Wright at the forefront of the designers of tall buildings and, as such, might have changed the direction of his entire professional career. Wright dedicated the design of this building to his late mentor Louis Sullivan.

Frank Lloyd Wright's home life and personal circumstances

A few days before his death in April, Louis Sullivan gave Wright a collection of original drawings: exquisite freehand sketches for buildings, ornamental details, as well as studies of nudes made while he was at the Ecole des Beaux-Arts in Paris. The end of Sullivan's life found him in poverty and these drawings were about the only personal items he had left. When he presented Wright with them he told him he would be writing about them sometime—he did a quarter century later in *Genius and the Mobocracy*. Sullivan also presented Wright with the first copy of his autobiography and inscribing it to him, he remarked, "Frank, it is you who has created the new architecture in America, but I do not believe you could have done it without me."

Frank Lloyd Wright's personal life took a turn for the better in November 1924 while visiting his friend, the painter Jerome Blum. One evening they went to the Russian ballet and, while waiting for the performance to start, a striking young woman with long black hair caught up into a bun took the last seat in their box. As luck would have it, Blum had met her at a dinner party in New York not too long before. She was Olga Ivanovna Milano Lazovich Hinzenberg (known as Olgivanna), a dancer

1924 BUILDINGS

Mabel and Charles Ennis
Residence, Los Angeles,
California. (*Left.*)

Nakoma Country Club,
Madison, Wisconsin.

Planetarium, Sugar Loaf
Mountain, Maryland.

PROJECTS
Gladney House, Fort Worth,
Texas.
Nakoma Country Club,
Madison, Wisconsin.
National Life Insurance
Company Skyscraper,
Chicago, Illinois.
Planetarium, Sugar Loaf
Mountain, Maryland.

from a patrician Montenegrin family who had been educated in Tsarist Russia and who possessed interesting and advanced social ideas. Frank was obviously attracted to her but this time the relationship would blossom into something very special. Throughout the autumn of 1924 Frank ardently pursued her.

It transpired that they were both waiting for a divorce, and Olgivanna was further fighting for custody of her daughter Svetlana. In fact, her husband pursued her to Chicago to contest the possession of their daughter.

Frank Lloyd Wright writings & publications

In The Cause of Architecture: In the Wake of the Quake; Concerning the Imperial Hotel, Tokio, published in *The Western Architect* (February). This was the second of a two-part essay (see F. L. W. writings, 1923).

Louis Henry Sullivan: Beloved Master, published in *The Western Architect* (June).
This is Wright's tribute to his "Lieber Meister." It begins: "The beloved master who knew how to be a great friend is dead. My young mind turned to him . . . and now, at middle age, I am to miss him and look back upon a long and loving association to which no new days, no new experiences may be added." It concludes with Wright's promise: "Later when I have more in perspective, I intend to write about and illustrate his work. It is too soon, now. I hope to make clear in unmistakable concrete terms, what is now necessarily abstract. A privilege I feel as mine and one I know from him that he would be pleased that I should take, as I have assured him I sometime would do."

Wright kept his promise a quarter-century later with *Genius and the Mobocracy*.

Left: Mabel and Charles Ennis Residence.

Mabel & Charles Ennis Residence

2655 Glendower Avenue, Los Angeles, California

Detached Chauffeur's Quarters.
Open for tours on the second Saturday of each odd month
by reservation only.

The monumental Ennis House, resembling a Mayan temple, was
Wright's largest and most elaborate commission in pre-cast concrete textile blocks. The site, occupying approximately one and a
half acres, was on a steep mound at the base of the Santa
Monica Mountains commanding spectacular views over the city
of Los Angeles. Wright's plan was for two buildings—the main
house and a chauffeur's apartment and garage—separated by a
paved courtyard. Constructed of sixteen-inch square blocks
joined by metal rods, Ennis House rises in stages from an enormous platform buttressed by a retaining wall.

*Right: Intricately leaded art-glass
windows were designed by Wright
for the interior.*

*Below: The house commands
spectacular views.*

Entry is below the main level and on the north side of the house the 100-foot long loggia links the main rooms and sets them open to the panoramic view of the city below. The dining room, a half-level further up, looks south. This level also features a guest room, pantry, and kitchen.

The division of the facade into zones of smooth and patterned blocks is continued on the interior walls, while geometric patterns in the art glass are redolent of the architect's earlier Prairie Houses. Teak provides contrast to the neutral blocks and the art-glass windows—abstractions of wisteria—are the last designed by Wright for domestic use.

As in the other Californian textile-block houses Ennis House was not without its problems. When parts of the south wall began to bulge and crack, Charles Ennis personally assumed control of the construction and he and his wife made several structural modifications. Charles Ennis died in 1926 but his wife Mabel occupied the house until 1936, when thereafter it changed hands on numerous occasions. In 1940, Ennis House was sold to the media personality John Nesbitt, who added a swimming pool and billiard room. In 1968 Mr. and Mrs. August Brown became the building's eighth owners and they replaced a bath, bedroom, and stucco wall with a Japanese garden, opposite the swimming pool.

With structural deficiencies too expensive to correct fully, the building was in a dilapidated state by the 1980s when Mr. Brown established the Trust for Preservation of Cultural Heritage to insure maintenance of the house in perpetuity. He donated the house to this nonprofit corporation and its longest-term tenant changed its name to Ennis-Brown in recognition of the contributions to its restoration.

*Above, left and far left: Ennis
House interiors.*

1925

Wright's move to the West Coast of America in 1923 had been short-lived and he returned to Chicago barely two years later.

Frank Lloyd Wright's home life and personal circumstances

Within three months of meeting her, Frank and Olgivanna were lovers and she had moved into Taliesin. In the spring, disaster visited Taliesin again when an electrical storm started a fire in some faulty wiring and the living quarters were razed to the ground by the conflagration. Rebuilding Taliesin again piled up more debt for Wright at a time when little work was around.

Olgivanna had obtained a divorce and Frank hoped to divorce Miriam. Matters became more urgent when Olgivanna discovered she was pregnant and, in December, gave birth to a daughter, Iovanna.

Frank Lloyd Wright writings & publications

Wright wrote three articles for the Dutch publication *Wendingen*. One of them was a description of the construction of the Imperial Hotel, Tokyo—*Facts Regarding the Imperial Hotel Dimension*. Although it was written before the Kanto earthquake of 1923, this was the first time it appeared in print. The other two articles he wrote for the magazine in 1925 were *In the Cause of Architecture: The Third Dimension* (in this essay Wright first used the term Usonia for the United States and its culture) and a special concluding message, *To My European Co-Workers*.

1925 BUILDINGS

Taliesin III (rebuilding of living quarters), Spring Green, Wisconsin. (*Left.*)

PROJECTS
Millard Gallery, Pasadena, California.
Phi Gamma Delta Fraternity House, University of Wisconsin, Madison, Wisconsin.
"Steel Cathedral," New York.

Taliesin III. Rebuilding "Taliesin North"

Spring Green, Wisconsin

Tours available April to December.
The current Taliesin was built in 1925 after fire destroyed
much of Taliesin I (1911) and II (1914).

In April 1925, during an electrical storm, lightning struck Taliesin
and short-circuited a new telephone system Wright had installed
in the house and set off a fire. Fanned by the high winds that
accompanied the storm, the fire was soon out of control. The
living quarters were lost but a dramatic change of wind direction and heavy rain saved the studio and workrooms.

Wright lost a number of priceless art treasures but the
insured building could be reconstructed. Taliesin had grown
piecemeal as the need to expand had arisen and now Wright
had the opportunity to design to a new orderly, unified plan.
After the fire Wright made forty sheets of pencil studies in pursuit of his latest vision for Taliesin reborn but rebuilding it for a
third time proved a tremendous drain on his financial resources.

*Right and below: After the 1925
fire, Wright executed extensive
westward additions.*

Constructed mostly of
native limestone, wood, and
plaster surfacing, it has been
continually altered over the
years, in keeping with the
needs of the Wrights and the
Taliesin Fellowship. After the
1925 fire, Wright planned and
executed extensive westward
additions. The hill garden was
partially terraced and a formal
terrace was completed south of
the architect's bedroom.

There was another fire at
Taliesin in February 1927, again

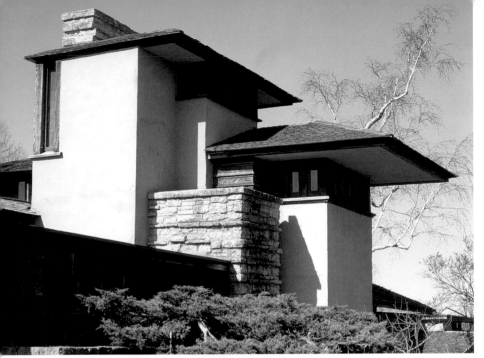

caused by faulty wiring. This was a minor fire but it was fortuitous for Wright as it delayed foreclosure on the property while the bank totaled up its losses and made a new appraisal.

The Taliesin Fellowship Complex was founded in 1933 as a school for architects and one of the first apprentices was John H. Howe. Various buildings were created or remodeled for the Fellowship, including the Drafting Studio (1922), Playhouse (1933 and rebuilt after the fire in 1952 as the Theater), the Midway Barns (1938), and Dairy and Machine Sheds (1947), all of which helped house, feed, and nurture his community. Fellows at the Taliesin Complex ate food provided by the rich Wisconsin soil at the working agricultural estate. The dams in the valley have created a small lake that is used for recreation as well as to control water flow through the farmland. Later the barns and the dairy sheds provided accommodation for the expanding architectural community of Taliesin.

The garden was built for Mrs. Wright by the Fellowship in the summer of 1960. Now preserved and run by the Foundation, the Taliesin Preservation Commission oversees the buildings that encompass the complex including:

1. Romeo and Juliet Windmill (1896)
2. Andrew Porter House (1907)
3. Taliesin (I 1911, II 1914, III 1925)
4 Taliesin Fellowship Complex
5. Taliesin Visitors' Center/River View Terrace Restaurant

Taliesin is one of the seventeen buildings designated to be retained by the AIA.

1926

In February Frank and his then wife, Miriam Noel, were await-
ing an impending divorce hearing. Wright's attorney reluctantly
admitted that his client was "insolvent" and this led to the Bank
of Wisconsin to solicit a new mortgage that would cover everything the architect owned. Judge James Hill, a lawyer and old
friend of Wright, advised him to go to the Bank of Wisconsin to
solicit a new mortgage for Taliesin. M. A. Mikkelsen, the editor
of the *Architectural Record*, was sympathetic to Wright's work and
mission and commissioned the architect to write five articles,
paying him five hundred dollars for each one written. These
earnings brought Wright much-needed revenue at a time when
he was especially financially pressed.

Frank Lloyd Wright's home life and personal circumstances
The financial demands of his second wife and the virulent press
attacks on his "scandalous lifestyle" forced Wright to go into hid-
ing with Olgivanna. On the advice of close friends they quietly
withdrew from Wisconsin and, in the summer, moved to a cottage in Minneapolis where they lived for a time under assumed
names. But such flagrant immorality offended many potential
clients and Wright found his commissions rapidly drying up. By
now Frank Lloyd Wright's career seemed at an end. There was a
popular misconception that he was one of the establishment figures in architecture, unable to keep up with contemporary
developments in the building world.

1926 PROJECTS

Kinder Symphony Playhouse,
    Oak Park, Illinois.
Standardized Concrete and
    Copper Gas Station.

1927

Frank Lloyd Wright's home life and personal circumstances

There was another fire at Taliesin in February, again caused by faulty wiring. This was a minor fire but it was fortuitous for Wright as it delayed foreclosure on the property while the bank totaled up its losses and made a new appraisal.

With nothing much to occupy him, Wright again took up writing and at the prompting of Olgivanna, started an autobiography and began preparing an exhibition of his work that would tour Europe and the United States. Money was still very much a problem for Wright so he sent a number of his Japanese prints to auction in New York. The sale helped to reduce his debts, but expenses continued to mount and his financial affairs got so bad that he was forced to turn Taliesin and the remains of his art collections over to the bank.

Frank moved to New York with Olgivanna, to stay with his sister Maginel, who was pursuing a successful career as an artist and author of children's books, after Taliesin had been threatened to be repossessed by the bank. With his terrible debts and no architectural work, his principle earnings came from *The Architectural Record*, whose editor had commissioned him to write the series *In the Cause of Architecture*.

Wright took the prudent step of engaging La Follette, member of a prominent Wisconsin family, as his lawyer in his dealings with the Bank of Wisconsin when it looked like he might lose Taliesin. La Follette played a heroic and largely thankless role in Wright's life at this time, as it was his duty to remind Frank what he could and could not do. (La Follette later went on to serve two terms as Governor of Wisconsin).

Olgivanna was in jeopardy of being deported because of problems with her visa but when the courts threatened to expel her from the country several of Wright's influential friends, led by Senator Henry J. Allen (former governor of Kansas), were

1927 BUILDINGS

Beach Cottages, Dumyât, Egypt.

Arizona Biltmore Hotel, Phoenix, Arizona (with Albert McArthur). (*Right.*)

D. D. Martin House "Graycliff," Derby, New York.

able to secure her safe refuge in the United States. Wright's messy divorce case with Miriam Noel finally came to an end when the decree was eventually granted in Madison on August 26, 1927.

Frank Lloyd Wright writings & publications

Why the Japanese Earthquake Did Not Destroy the Imperial Hotel, published in *Liberty* (December).

The Collection of Japanese Antique Prints, published as a catalogue by The Anderson Galleries, New York.
This was a substantive introduction to the sales catalogue.

M. A. Mikkelsen, the editor of *The Architectural Record*, commissioned Wright to write a five articles under the title he used in 1908 and again in 1914, *In the Cause of Architecture*. Mikklesen then extended the commission to include a further nine articles the following year. *The Architectural Record* began publishing the series in May 1927, with:

In the Cause of Architecture 1: The Architect and the Machine. This is Wright's view of the machine as beneficial or destructive, depending upon how it was to be understood and used.

In the Cause of Architecture II: Standardization, the Soul of the Machine (June).
"Standardization apprehended as a principle of order has the danger of monotony in application. Standardization can be murderer or beneficent factor as the life in the thing standardized is kept by imagination or destroyed by the lack of it."

In the Cause of Architecture III: Steel (August)
"Steel is the epic of this age. Steel has entered our lives as a 'material' to take upon itself the physical burden of our civilisation."

In the Cause of Architecture IV: Fabrication and Imagination (October).
"Time was when the hand wrought. Time is here when the process fabricated instead. Why make the fabrication a lie or allow it to become one when we try to make it beautiful? Any such lie is an abuse of Imagination."

In the Cause of Architecture V: The New World (October)
"Idealism and Idealist are the same failure as Realism and Realistic. Both the same failure as Romance and Romantic. Life is. We are."

Left and far left: Arizona Biltmore Hotel

Arizona Biltmore Hotel

East Sahuaro Drive, Camino Acequia, Phoenix, Arizona

Fifteen cottages:
Six single-story, type 1, cottages (four apartment)
Five single-story, type 2, cottages (five apartment)
Four two-story cottages
Guided tours by appointment.

The hotel was probably the largest of Wright's "textile-block" designs, although there is some debate about how much of the design was his. The complex of buildings is recognized as the result of collaboration between Wright and Albert Chase McArthur, a former draftsman in the Oak Park Studio. The job architect, McArthur, who was interested in using Wright's concrete-block construction system, called him in to act as a consultant. When Wright left Phoenix, McArthur made changes

Below: The hotel is a collaboration between Wright and Albert Chase McArthur.

in Wright's proportions. He deemed four floors better than three, or three than two, wherever possible. Within months of the hotel opening, in February 1929, McArthur was trying to dispel any rumours that Wright had, in fact, been the architect. In April 1930, he finally asked Wright for a formal statement, which clarified to all the exact nature of the relationship *vis à vis* the Biltmore. In June 1930, Wright, who considered the building "even worse" than he thought it would be, replied in writing stating, "Albert McArthur is the architect of that building—all attempts to take credit for that performance are gratuitous and beside the mark."

Above: The hotel is probably one of the largest of Wright's textile-block designs.

Overleaf: The lobby is reminiscent of the Imperial Hotel, Wright's demolished Japanese venture.

However, much of the detail work bears his hallmarks—particularly the patterned concrete blocks, the lobby (which is reminiscent of the Imperial Hotel, Wright's demolished Japanese venture), the adjoining single and two-story cottages, and the fabulous multi-colored glass mural adapted from a design in *Liberty* magazine.

The complex occupies 200 acres of a proposed 621-acre development in the foothills of Squaw Peak and had its own water system and underground electrical facilities, the first such in Arizona. It also had a nursery growing fresh vegetables and fruits for the hotel restaurants.

In the front, the entrance wing projects from the main four-story block, which contains the lobby, dining room, and sun room on the first floor, with guest rooms on the upper levels. The grandeur of the lobby is complimented by the second-floor balcony and a ceiling covered in gold leaf. The copper roof consists of 32,500 pounds of Sun Belt copper. The green-stained, concrete floor has an incised motif that corresponds to the dimensions of the unit blocks, which are not organized on the sixteen-inch module, as recommended by Wright, but on blocks that measure eighteen inches by thirteen inches, which was McArthur's idea.

As in Wright's Californian textile-block houses, patterned and plain blocks are combined but, unlike the angular, abstract patterns that Wright had employed, McArthur used blocks patterned with subtle curves in both perforated and solid versions. To the rear of the hotel, two wings extend and partially enclose a hexagonal patio. One of the wings houses the polygonal ballroom in which ten large beams rise like the spokes of a great wheel to support the roof.

When the hotel opened for its second season in November 1929, just after the great stock market crash, one of the stockholders, William Wrigley Jr. (of the chewing gum empire), was the effective owner. Wrigley died in 1932, but the Biltmore and surrounding estates remained in the Wrigley family, guided by the only son Philip, until 1973. The hotel was renovated after a fire in June 1973. Additions, by Taliesin Associated Architects, have been made using textile block to blend old with new.

Right : The hotel was renovated after a fire in June 1973.

1928

Around this time a number of Frank Lloyd Wright's friends and former clients formed Frank Lloyd Wright Inc., a scheme to bankroll the great architect, keep him from debt, and make his return to Taliesin possible.

The prospect of work had at last appeared in 1927 when Wright was asked by the McArthur family to act as consultant on the building of the Arizona Biltmore Hotel. While staying for three months in Phoenix, he met Dr. Alexander Chandler, the owner of a large hotel and founder and owner of much of the town of Chandler. He wanted to build a large, elegant, hotel-cum-resort in the desert outside Chandler, where the rich could escape the rigors of winter. This project was called San Marcos-in-the-Desert, and Wright lived on the site for a time before moving to La Jolla in California.

Frank Lloyd Wright's home life and personal circumstances
Finally, on August 25, 1928, Frank and Olgivanna married in a quiet ceremony in the garden of an inn in Rancho Santa Fe. The marriage provided Frank with a stability that allowed him to focus his energies in spite of the few commissions during the years of the great depression.

1928 BUILDINGS

Ocatillo Desert Camp, Chandler, Arizona (Wright's temporary southwestern headquarters).

PROJECTS
Beach Cottages, Ras-el-Bar Island, Dumyât, Egypt.
Blue Sky Burial Terraces, Buffalo, New York.
Cudney House, Chandler, Arizona.
Jones House I, Tulsa, Oklahoma.
Low-cost concrete block houses, Chandler, Arizona.
San Marcos in the Desert Resort Hotel, Chandler, Arizona.
San Marcos Water Gardens, Chandler, Arizona.
School, La Jolla, California.
Young House, Chandler, Arizona.

Ocattillo Desert Camp

Chandler, Arizona

Demolished: c. 1929
The site remains with some evidence of Wright's occupancy.

Ocatillo (Wright spelled it "Ocatilla") was a temporary encampment, constructed of wood and canvas, established by Wright while working on the San Marcos-in-the-Desert project for Dr. Alexander Chandler. Ocatillo, or "candle flame," is a cactus with long slender spires of green, topped by brilliant red blossoms. The name "candle flame," was given to the red triangular forms created by the one-two (thirty-sixty degree) triangle, and painted in the gables. The camp consisted of a group of buildings around a hill, with a board-and-batten wall to link them and enclose the area against any outside dangers. The indoor areas were covered by white canvas that diffused the brilliant desert sun creating a magical effect. The result was so successful that it became the prototype for Taliesin West.

Frank Lloyd Wright writings & publications

These are the extended commissions for *The Architectural Record* (see F. L. W writings, 1927).

In The Cause of Architecture: I. The Logic of the Plan (January)
A seminal essay in which Wright attempted to establish his architectural philosophy. He stressed the importance of limiting the number of spaces to those that were necessary, and eliminating any unnecessary ornamentation and detail: "Plan! There is something elemental in the word itself. A pregnant plan has logic—is the logic of the building squarely stated. Unless it is the plan for a foolish fair."

In The Cause of Architecture: II. What "Styles" Mean to the Architect (February).
"Styles once accomplished soon become yardsticks for the blind, crutches for the lame, the recourse of the impotent. As humanity develops there will be less recourse for 'style' and more style . . . "

In The Cause of Architecture: III. The Meaning of Materials—Stone (April).
"For in the stony bonework of the Earth, the principles that shaped stone as it lies, or as it rises and remains to be sculpted by winds and tide—there sleep forms and styles enough for all the ages, for all of Man."

In the Cause of Architecture IV: The Meaning of Materials—Wood (May).
"No Western peoples ever used wood with such understanding as the Japanese did in their construction—where wood always came up and came out as nobly beautiful."

In the Cause of Architecture V: The Meaning of Materials—The Kiln (June).
"It appears from a glance the oven is as old as civilization at least—which is old enough for us."

In the Cause of Architecture VI: The Meaning of Materials—Glass
(July).
"Perhaps the greatest difference eventually between ancient and modern buildings will be due to our modern machine-made glass. Glass, in any wide utilitarian sense, is new."

In the Cause of Architecture VII: The Meaning of Materials—Concrete
(August).
This was Wright's defense of the "inferior" building material—concrete.

In the Cause of Architecture VIII: Sheet Metal and a Modern Instance
(October).
"The Machine is at its best when rolling, cutting, stamping, or folding whatever may be fed into it."

In the Cause of Architecture IX: The Terms
Wright's conclusions to his *In the Cause of Architecture series*.

Toward a New Architecture published in *World Unity* (September).
Wright's scathing attack on Le Corbusier.

Fiske Kimball's New Book published in the *Architectural Record* (August).
Wright's damning criticism of Fiske Kimball's book *American Architecture*.

1929

As 1929 began, the year of the great stock market crash, Wright was commissioned by the Rosenwald Foundation to design one of the schoolhouses that this philanthropic organization was building for underprivileged black children in the town. This was also the time when Wright signed a life contract with the Leerdam Glass-fabriek of Holland to design on a royalty basis.

The stock market crash brought all Wright's commissions to an abrupt halt, including, most notably, the San Marcos-in-the-Desert project. The only work he was left with was a large house he was building for his cousin Richard Lloyd Jones, in Tulsa, Oklahoma.

Frank Lloyd Wright's home life and personal circumstances

In the winter of 1929, with his family and followers, Wright returned to the Ocatillo Camp in the Arizona Desert. They stayed in the temporary town built out of canvas and boxboards while Frank was working on the San Marcos project. Wright liked the place so much that the camp became the prototype for the winter home he would design in 1937 for the Taliesin Fellowship—Taliesin West in Scottsdale, Arizona.

1929 BUILDINGS

Richard Lloyd Jones House II "Westhope," Tulsa, Oklahoma. (*Left.*)

St. Marks in the Bowrie, New York City, New York.

PROJECTS
St. Marks Tower, New York.

Frank Lloyd Wright writings & publications
Surface and Mass—Again! Published in *The Architectural Record* (July).
The European work in modern architecture at this time was being lauded in the United States under the heading the "International Style." Its pioneering practitioners were Le Corbusier, Walter Gropius, and Mies van der Rohe. Wright disliked their buildings, he considered them bare, sterile, and boxlike—devoid of the "depth dimension." In this article, however, he is not so much attacking the European architects as he is the American critics.

Richard Lloyd Jones Residence

3704 South Birmingham Avenue, Tulsa, Oklahoma

Detached garage and servants' quarters.
Various alterations, including the addition of a concealed air-conditioning system, and several resizings of the kitchen.

Wright's concrete-block experiments of the 1920s were drawn to a close with this house designed for the architect's cousin, Richard Lloyd Jones. The four-acre plot overlooks the hills of the Arkansas River Valley and the Turkey Mountains.

Constructed from glass and "textile-block," the flat-roofed building was planned on a square grid. Although it is only two-stories high, for just one third of the plan, it houses six bedrooms, a library, and billiard room, as well as the usual dining room, living room, kitchen, and servants' quarters. In the design, that encloses a raised inner courtyard with pool, identi-

Below: The Lloyd Jones Residence is constructed from glass and textile-block.

cal concrete piers are alternated with panels of glass to create a rather severe fortress-like appearance. Built on a five-foot-square unit module, it employs dry-tamped concrete blocks inside and out, colored a dull orange-brown to blend with the local sandstone. The blocks are one-third by one-fourth of the module in surface dimension.

Inside, patterned perforated blocks are used to house recessed light fixtures and to hide heating vents. Typically, four plain blocks are stacked before the designed block is laid. The lights in the recessed grills are dipped in orange shellac to provide a candle-like glow.

Richard Lloyd Jones lived in the house until his death at age ninety. The building has since gone through various modifications and renovations, primarily by architect Murray McCune in 1965, then the Nelson family, and more recently Sandra Holden and Dr. Dwight Holden. The modifications have largely been to accommodate modern conveniences such as air-conditioning and new kitchen appliances. The open terrace has been made into an enclosed patio and the stairwell to the top floor, not on Wright's original plans, was added during construction.

Above: Concrete piers are alternatived with panels of glass.

Overleaf: A raised inner courtyard contains a pool.

1930/1

With work again scarce, Wright had to turn to writing and lecturing for the bulk of his income. Douglas Haskell, a writer for the *Architectural Record*, published a spirited defense of Wright in *The Nation* when it seemed that plans for the building of the Chicago World's Fair in 1933 would not include him. In the late spring of this year Wright was invited to give the famous Kahn Lectures on art, archaeology, and architecture at Princeton University (published in book form the following year). This gave him the privilege of mounting an exhibition of his work that would then travel around the country.

In 1931, Wright lectured at New York's New School for Social Research where he called for a reconsideration of the skyscraper, which he considered "the most typical product of the American civilization." He proposed that high-rise buildings should not crowd in upon each other as they did, but should occupy separate, park-like settings, widely spaced and easily accessible as both dwellings and workplaces. These ideas would manifest themselves later in Wright's Broadacre City concept.

In general Wright wasn't a very good teacher as his ideas were too individualistic for students to find useful.

1930 PROJECTS

Automobile with cantilevered top.
Cabins for desert or woods, YMCA, Chicago, Illinois.
Grouped apartment towers, Chicago, Illinois.
Noble Apartment House, Los Angeles, California.

Frank Lloyd Wright writings & publications

Architecture as a Profession is All Wrong, published
    in *The American Architect* (December).
Addressing the alarming state of architectural firms,
    Wright here condemns the growth and develop-
    ment of what he calls the "plan-factories."

In Order to be Modern, published in *Architectural
    Progress* (December).
This relatively short article summarizes all that Wright
    has been writing about for the past three and a
    half decades.

*The Logic of Contemporary Architecture as an
    Expression of this Age*, published in *The
    Architectural Forum* (May).

1931 PROJECTS

The Capital Journal Newspaper Building, Salem,
    Oregon.
"House on the Mesa," Denver, Colorado.
Three schemes for "A Century of Progress," World's
    Fair, Chicago, Illinois.

Frank Lloyd Wright writings & publications

Modern Architecture, the Kahn Lectures for 1930,
    Princeton University Press, 1931.

1932

Like most other architects at the time, the Great Depression left Wright with few commissions but instead of retiring at the age of sixty-five, he entered into a whole new era of creativity. With the encouragement he received and the general revival of interest following the publication of his autobiography, Wright established the Taliesin Fellowship at Spring Green, Wisconsin. It was started at the worst point of the Great Depression and was conceived along the lines of a utopian community of worker-apprentices who paid a fee to come and work and live with the great architect. Wright's friends, relatives, clients, and neighbors were all of the opinion that the school would not survive longer than a year. They were wrong and the community grew as apprentices arrived. Olgivanna Wright, who put into play her advanced social theories learned at the Gurdjieff Institute, created an almost mystical reverence and fostered much of their attitude. Wright was presented as the revered master at whose feet they were privileged to learn and pay homage.

Despite paying for the honor, part of the apprentices' daily routine was to do chores around the house and grounds, in between working on their assigned design projects. They helped to run the home and office and helped on many of his projects with drawings and model making, while some of them later went on to work for Wright on Taliesin West. It can be seen as a tribute to the Wrights and to the apprentices who, hand in hand, worked hard and long to keep Taliesin afloat. In time his best assistants were trusted with control of his projects and personal supervision of his work became a rarity rather than the norm. Three of the first apprentices were William Wesley Peters, John H. Howe, and Edgar Tafel, all of whom would go on to become noted architects in their own right.

1932 PROJECTS

Automobile and airplane filling and service station.
Movie House and shops, Michigan, Indiana.
Pre-fabricated sheet steel farm units.
Highway overpass.
New theater.
Overhead filling station.
Pre-fabricated sheet steel and glass roadside markets.
Willey House I, Minneapolis, Minnesota.

Frank Lloyd Wright writings & publications

An Autobiography, published by Longmans, Green and Company. This work, although shamelessly biased and self-promoting, stimulated new interest in Wright and his work.

The Disappearing City, published by William Fraquhar Payson, contained the original, if eccentric, idea of reserving an acre of land for every American at birth.

Taliesin Fellowship Complex

Hillside

Hillside Drafting Studio
Tours of the Fellowship Complex are offered daily during
the warmer months of the year.

Wright and his Fellowship apprentices undertook a major
expansion of the original laboratory classrooms of Hillside
School, the Dana Gallery, and Roberts Room at Taliesin. This
great hall of the drafting studio is across the bridge to the north
of the main entry to Taliesin. Henry-Russell Hitchcock referred to
the drafting studio as an "abstract forest" due to the density of
the open trusses, constructed from timber felled and sawn into
rough lumber by the apprentices. Along each side of the hall
were two rows of bedrooms for the apprentices. In 1978–80 the
hall was refurbished when the roof and trusses were removed
and rebuilt, opening the saw-
tooth clerestories. The nearly
constant reworking of the
school since 1902 has meant
that any renovations are
extremely expensive and com-
plicated. The Taliesin
Preservation Commission
administers the whole project
and the great drafting hall is
still a center of activity for the
Taliesin Associated Architects.

1933

A major problem of these Depression years was finding good quality, economic houses for middle-class families and this is where Wright came up with the concept of the "Usonian" house that would bring into full play new developments in building, in particular the use of pre-cast concrete. (Usonia was Wright's term for the United States and its culture. It was first used in his 1925 essay "In the Cause of Architecture: The Third Dimension" published in the Dutch *Wendingen*). This can be seen as Wright's fifth phase and the most productive in his long career. He foresaw such homes as being integral to his dream of a wide-spreading utopian development he called Broadacre City—a dream project he would work on for the remainder of his life.

Taliesin Fellowship Complex

Spring Green, Wisconsin

Hillside Playhouse, Hillside Theatre (1952)
Playhouse destroyed by fire, 1952, rebuilt as Hillside
Theatre.

Frank Lloyd Wright and the first Taliesin apprentices remodeled
the Hillside Home School II, converting the gymnasium into the
Hillside Playhouse, for use by the fellowship. The playhouse was
subsequently destroyed by fire in 1952 when Wright built a new
theater, giving it its own foyer. The theater also had the adjacent
classrooms converted to a new dining room at a balcony level to
the stage and overlooking it from behind.

1934

Construction of Taliesin West started in 1934 as a winter home for Wright and this was also the year in which Wright built his model for Broadacre City, the dream project of a utopian development he worked on for the latter part of his life. He envisioned whole communities where each family would live on an acre of land, hence the name, and was to be a development that considered social needs as well as personal ones. Broadacre City was not a model of buildings but rather a scheme for buildings, themselves represented by blocks, set into the countryside. The model described a four-square mile settlement to house 1,400 families and was organized by its transportation system and by "zones of activity." Highways and feeder roads were arranged to allow people to travel to their work or leisure activities with the minimum of inconvenience and in addition to small-scale manufacturing zones, the plans also included farming areas. A variety of housing types were offered with "cost saving houses," with glass roofs and roof gardens and were described as "prefabricated units."

Frank Lloyd Wright's home life and personal circumstances

G. I. Gurdjieff, philosopher and spiritual adviser to Olgivanna Lazovich Wright, first came to Taliesin in the summer of 1934. After his visit, Wright wrote a short essay comparing him to Gandhi and Whitman and praising his solid, fatherly manner. Gurdjieff was one of the few men Wright seemed to recognize as an equal.

1934 BUILDINGS

**Malcolm E. Willey House,
   Minneapolis, Minnesota.**
   (*Left.*)

PROJECTS
Broadacre City model and exhi-
   bition plans.
Willey House II.
Helicopter project.
Road machine project.
Train project.
Zoned House Number 1.

Malcolm E. Willey House

255 Bedford Street, Minneapolis, Minnesota

> During the winter months there are glimpses of this private house through the foliage in front of the living room and the bedrooms.

The house, constructed from dark red sand and paving brick, with cypress wood-trim, is located on a bluff above the Mississippi River. The use of cypress is important. Wright had always shown a preference for American woods, particularly oak, but its major fault was that its open grain easily retained dust and dirt, quickly darkening it. Cypress, particularly East Coast red tidewater cypress, became the preferred choice of wood for all Usonian construction. It was a beautiful looking wood, highly resistant to rot, with a fine grain and warm coloration.

The design for this single-story house, originally designed as a two-story house, marks a turning point in Wright's domestic architecture. The original two-story plans hark back to the Prairie House style but the built version looks forward to the houses of the future. This was the first house by Wright to have the kitchen joined to the living and dining areas —described by Wright as a "workspace." The building represents the major bridge between the Prairie Style and the soon-to-appear standard L-plan Usonian House.

All the features of a Usonian in-line plan are here but are not in the usual order. The workspace is on one side of the living room, and the gallery linking the quiet spaces on the other. This was an arrangement Wright employed in his first true in-line Usonian (the Lloyd Lewis Residence of 1939) but soon abandoned for a workspace at the junction of the living room and gallery, as in L-plan houses. There have been recent restorations to the interior and the brick terrace.

1935

In the 1930s, after the Depression, Wright introduced his Usonian House design—small, single, free-standing houses for "true Americans" or Usonians. "USONIA" was an acronym for the United States of North America which Wright first used in 1925—he credited Samuel Butler for its creation, but no one has yet been able to find the original quote. These houses were extremely inexpensive structures, constructed with walls of wooden sandwiches and flat roofs of crossed rough wooden beams. Wright's concept would bring into full play new developments in building, particularly the use of pre-cast concrete. The Usonian concept differs radically from previous types of Wright homes and is nowhere more apparent than in their plan and in the organization of interior space. These flat-roofed structures broke down the distinction between the outside and inside worlds, with walls and doors of glass that looked and opened out on to gardens. The interiors were infinitely flexible, with moveable screens instead of walls.

The Broadacre City model, after initially being exhibited at the Rockefeller Center, traveled to Pittsburgh, Washington, D.C., Madison, Iowa County, Marquette, and Michigan, before returning to Taliesin. The theme of his utopian city and its underlying ideas and principles, would return constantly throughout Wright's life, from the time the model was first built to his death.

1935 PROJECTS

Hoult House, Wichita, Kansas.
Lusk House, Huron, South Dakota.
Marcus House, Dallas, Texas.
Zoned City House.
Zoned Country House.
Zoned Suburban House.

Frank Lloyd Wright writings & publications

Broadacre City: A New Community Plan, published (April).

1936

The building of "Fallingwater" in Pennsylvania for Edgar Kaufmann in 1936 and the completion of the S. C. Johnson & Son Administration Building in Racine, Wisconsin (1936–39) saw a further upsurge in Wright's reputation. His confident incorporation of new building methods and materials impressed the new generation of up-and-coming architects.

The first Usonian House was built in 1936 for Herbert Jacobs in Madison, Wisconsin, and Wright would go on to build over a hundred more.

Frank Lloyd Wright's home life and personal circumstances

Wright was again in Phoenix, Arizona, recovering from a bout of pneumonia when Olgivanna encouraged him to think about building a permanent home in the desert, one to which he, his family, and the Taliesin Fellowship could migrate each winter from the unbearable cold of Wisconsin.

Frank Lloyd Wright writings & publications

In an article for the *Architects' Journal of London*, Wright expounded his idea that the future of architecture was an integration of nature with the potentiality of the machine for a more fully human civilization, "The proper use of the machine should be to make life more beautiful, more livable. No, not necessarily easier or quicker just to feed this American voracity which we call speed. If speed and destruction plus sanitation are to be the function of machinery among us, the machine will destroy us and its present idolatory will eventually defeat our attempt at a culture."

1936 BUILDINGS

Herbert Jacobs House, Madison, Wisconsin. (*Right*.)

S. C. Johnson Wax Company Administration Building, Racine, Wisconsin.

Edgar Kaufmann House "Fallingwater," Bear Run, Pennsylvania.

Abby Beecher Roberts House "Deertrack," Marquette, Michigan.

PROJECTS

Little San Marcos in the Desert Resort Inn, Chandler, Arizona.

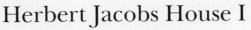

Herbert Jacobs House I

441 Toepfer Street, Madison, Wisconsin

Front elevation visible from the street.

Despite the construction of the Willey House (1934), this building is considered by many to be the first Usonian House and in fact Wright called it Usonia I. It gained almost instant acclaim, largely because of its low cost at a time when America was emerging from the Great Depression. Many young couples wanted to have the opportunity to become the owners of an affordable house. The original cost of the house was $5,500. It is certainly the first design that separated the bedrooms from the living areas in a separate wing, abolished the dining room as a separate enclosed space, and utilized a planning grid incised into the concrete floor. It demonstrated Wright's complete rethinking of the small house. Wright exploited the potential of

the small site by turning the back of the house onto the street and organizing the building around an L-shaped courtyard, instead of simply scaling down in size the traditional urban house. The active and quiet spaces are joined by a 90-degree angle, creating a typical L-plan with the whole drawn on a grid of two-by-four-foot rectangles. The living room is one-third of the 1,560 square foot plan.

The masonry is brick and the dry wall employs horizontal recessed three-inch redwood battens with nine-inch pine boards screwed onto a core of vertical pine boards. When the house was discovered for sale in the 1980s, the exterior walls were black with creosote that has now been chemically removed in preference to replacing the boards, which were provided by the California Redwood Association free of charge.

Its current owner has lovingly restored the house. The original roof and several layers of asphalt have been replaced with a rubber-membrane roof provided without charge from Celotex Corp. Restoration, under project architect John A. Eifler. The house is listed on the National Register of Historic Places.

Right: Dining room.

Below: The exterior has been restored to its previous appearance.

S. C. Johnson and Co. Building

1525 Howe Street, Racine, Wisconsin

Additions (1951)
Research Tower, Heliolaboratory (1944)
Free public tours are given regularly (by reservation only).

Wright is best known for his residential work, but the Johnson Wax Building also puts him at the forefront of commercial design. This building contains many unusual and innovative features, the best-known being the slender, dendriform columns in the central hypostyle hall that are capable of supporting six times the weight imposed on them. The columns caused great controversy at the time. In fact, the State Building inspectors stopped construction in order to perform a full-scale test to determine their permissible and ultimate carrying weights. The columns were designed to support twelve tons but when they were tested they were able to hold sixty tons, unsurprisingly the building inspectors allowed construction to continue. The idea for these columns was first proposed five years earlier in unexecuted designs for a newspaper building in Salem, Oregon.

The building has no plate glass windows, only Pyrex glass tubes to admit light. The use of lighting tubes of differing diameters in horizontal bands, set in conjunction with a brick facing to admit light during the day and illumination at night, provides brilliant warmth to the interior. At night the roof appears to float above the red brick walls.

The interior of the Administration Building is unusual, creating an effect like that of looking through a small grove of concrete trees. The space is very large but the columns create differing effects, at times making it seem larger and at others smaller—a visual feature typical of many of Wright's designs. As with many of the architect's projects, the furniture is an integral part of the whole. Most of the chairs for those working on the main floor were three-legged without wheeled castors and had

pivoted backs. The colors of their original fabric included the familiar Cherokee red of the floor and brick, along with a soft blue, green, and yellow ochre. The original Cherokee red rubber tiles of the floor are now covered with carpet.

The Administration Building and the Tower are generally recognized as two of the most remarkable structures of the interwar period and have been designated by the AIA as two of the seventeen buildings designed by Wright to be retained as supreme examples of his architectural contribution to American culture.

Above, left and right: Interior of S.C. Johnson and Son Building.

Edgar J. Kaufmann House

Mill Run, State Highway 381, Pennsylvania

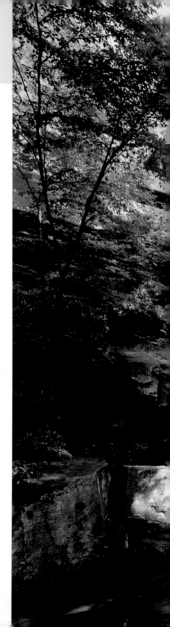

The Western Pennsylvania Conservancy conducts guided tours throughout the year; these are limited to weekends during the cold winter months. Reservations are advised.

The Kaufmanns owned a tract of land, which included a stream called Bear Run, in the mountains some 60 miles south of Pittsburgh. Although the family used to camp on the site in summer, they now wanted a year-round house. "Fallingwater," Wright's masterpiece for Edgar and Liliane Kaufmann, has to be the architect's most important and grandest domestic commission of the 1930s and is perhaps the best-known private home for someone not of royal blood in the history of architecture. In 1936 Wright further developed his "organic" philosophy in "Fallingwater," an extraordinary cantilevered house in an idyllic setting. It is based on forms borrowed from nature, and the intentions were clearly romantic, poetic, and intensely personal. This is arguably the closest Wright came to the realization of his romantic vision of man living in total harmony with nature. When Wright visited the site at Bear Run he noticed a large smooth boulder overhanging a waterfall and told his clients that he wanted them to "live with the waterfall" as an "integral part" of their lives. The house is boldly cantilevered over this waterfall and anchored with a series of reinforced concrete "trays" attached to the masonry wall and natural rock forming the rear of the house. These trays appear to float weightlessly above the valley floor.

Pottsville sandstone quarried on site, concrete, and glass form the exterior and interior fabric of the building. The feeling of nature is achieved internally by carrying the character of the stonework in floors and walls in opposition to the trees that can be seen surrounding the building through the almost uninterrupted glass and wrap-round corner windows. The first-floor entry, the living room, and the dining room are integrated to form a continuous space. A hatch opening to a suspended stairway allowed for ventilation and provided access to the stream below the house, while the upper floors accommodate the bedrooms, which open onto private terraces.

In October 1963, "Fallingwater" was presented by Edgar Kaufmann Jnr. to the Western Pennsylvania Conservancy, together with 1,543 acres of surrounding land. The inventiveness that Wright showed in all aspects of the design ensures that "Fallingwater" occupies a unique place in modern architectural history and is one of seventeen buildings designated by the American Institute of Architects to be retained as an example of the architect's contribution to American culture.

Below and left: Interiors showing panoramic views.

1937

Wright had always been an outspoken critic of most other architects, and this held true when his reputation revived and grew greater during the 1930s. Such younger American architects as Philip Johnson and Henry-Russell Hitchcock coined the term International Style to describe the European architects they admired most—Le Corbusier, Gropius, and Mies van der Rohe. Wright belittled the style and announced that its proponents had copied him.

Frank Lloyd Wright writings & publications

Architecture and Modern Life (with Baker Brownell), published by Harper and Brothers.

1937 BUILDINGS

Bramson Dress Shop, Oak Park, Illinois.

Paul Hanna House, "Honeycomb House," Stanford, California.

Herbert F. Johnson House, "Wingspread," Wind Point, Wisconsin.

Edgar J. Kaufmann Sr. Offices, Pittsburgh, Pennsylvania (now in the Victoria & Albert Museum in London). (*Left.*)

Ben Rebhuhn House, Great Neck Estates, Long Island, New York.

PROJECTS
100 All Steel Houses, Los Angeles, California.
Borglum Studio, Black Hills, South Dakota.
Bramson Dress Shop, Oak Park, Illinois.
"Memorial to the Soil" Chapel, Southern Wisconsin.
Garage for Parker House, Janesville, Wisconsin.

Paul R. and Jean Hanna House

737 Frenchman's Road, Stanford, California

Workshop addition (1950)
Residence alterations (1957)
The house is open for visits on a limited basis.

The Hanna residence completes the hillside to which it clings, its floor and courtyard levels adjusting to the contours of the hill. While generally considered Usonian, the eventual size and cost—which greatly exceeded the cost of $15,000—of the Hanna House was beyond the means of most Americans at the time. Nevertheless, the grid plan, the interior and exterior walls of board-and-batten construction, and the central location of the kitchen workspace are characteristics shared by all of the Usonian Houses. It is brick-built in common wire-cut San Jose brick but many of the internal walls are wood and were

Right: The floor of the house adjusts to the contours of the hill.

Below right: Detail of exterior terrace.

Below: The house has unrestricted views enhanced by large amounts of glass opening out on to the brick terraces.

designed to be moveable—especially to change the layout of the playroom as the owners' children grew up. Wright called this a wooden house. In this house Wright abandoned the square or rectangle as the basic unit for both the grid and the plan in favor of the hexagon. Thus giving the house its popular name, the "Honeycombe House." With walls joined at 120-degree angles, a fluid interior space and unrestricted views are created, further enhanced by the large amounts of glass that open out on to the brick terraces and the hillside providing additional outdoor living spaces.

The living room and workspace are unchanged since original construction, but Wright altered most of the rest of the house. There was major damage ($1.8m worth) to the house in 1989 during the Loma Prieta earthquake. The Hanna House is one of seventeen buildings designated by the American Institute of Architects to be retained as an example of Wright's contribution to American culture and is now maintained by Stanford University.

Herbert F. Johnson House

33 East Four Mile Road, Wind Point, Wisconsin

No access to the public. However, the house and grounds are accessible to those participating in the foundation's programs.

Wright designed "Wingspread" for Herbert F. Johnson of Johnson Wax and it is one of the few large houses he designed for a wealthy client, yet is one of his best. The architect himself called the Johnson House the "last of the Prairie Houses" and considered it to be his best and most expensive house to date. Wright called the house "Wingspread" because the plan consisted of four wings extended in a pinwheel fashion from a high-ceilinged, polygonal central space (which the architect likened to a wigwam), housing an enormous chimney with five fireplaces on two levels. At the point where the chimney

Left and below: The house consists of four wings that extend in a pinwheel fashion.

emerged through the sloping, tiled roof, Wright placed a small glass observatory. The central space, accessed from the low entrance vestibule, is one of the architect's finest interiors and acts as a focus to the four wings of the house, one containing the master bedrooms, others guest and children's rooms, the services and garages.

Pink Kasota sandstone, red brick, and cypresses are the primary construction materials. The interior is finished in oak rather than the darker American walnut used in the owner's company's Administration Building. Inside the warm brick and oak tones are enriched by light from three bands of clerestory windows, set into a circle round the roof. The deep brick fins make the interior space appear very open from the inside, and the exterior dark and secluded from the outside. The focal point of the living space remains the "sacred hearth," the "heart" of the home.

Despite being converted into seminar rooms for the current occupants—The Johnson Foundation—the wings retain many details from the original structure. The building, in particular the clerestory of the central pavilion, has recently undergone extensive structural work.

Above, left and right: Interior of Johnson House.

1938

Half of the buildings from Wright's imagination that were still standing in 1973 were created by 1938, though half of his thousand-plus projects would not be on the drawing boards until the end of World War II.

Wright's winter home for the Taliesin Fellowship was Taliesin West, a complex of buildings, which included a theater, music pavilion, and Sun Cottage and offered a new challenge in building materials. He first started work on the site in 1938 with apprentices from Taliesin North. Every winter for the next twenty-two years, he and his students would continue the work by revising and enlarging the complex.

Frank Lloyd Wright writings & publications

Life Presents in Collaboration with the Architectural Forum Eight Houses For Modern Living Especially Designed by Famous American Architects for Four Representative Families Earning $2,000 to $10,000 a Year published in *Life* in September.

1938 BUILDINGS

Florida Southern College, Lakeland, Florida (construction through 1959).
Administration Building: 1945.
Danforth Chapel: 1954. *(Left)*
Industrial Arts Building: 1942.
Pfeiffer Chapel: 1938.
Roux Library: 1941.
Science Building: 1953.
Seminar Buildings: 1940.

Monona Terrace, Madison, Wisconsin.

Taliesin West, Scottsdale, Arizona (Wright's winter headquarters).

PROJECTS

Jester All-Plywood Houses, Palos Verde, California (design constructed by Bruce Brooks Pfeiffer, Director of Archives at the Foundation, in the grounds of Taliesin West, Scottsdale, Arizona, 1971).

Johnson Gatehouse and Farm Group, Wind Point, Wisconsin.

Jargensen House, Evanston, Illinois.

McCallum House, Northampton, Massachusetts.

Monona Terrace, Madison Civic Center, Wisconsin (building commenced in 1994 based on revised plans from 1959. Opening planned for late 1997).

Smith House (Pine Tree) Piedmont Pines, California.

Florida Southern College

South Johnson Avenue at Lake Hollingworth Drive, Lakeland, Florida

The site is open to the public.
Annie Merner Pfeiffer Chapel.
Stage enlarged, seating reduced. Air-conditioning added,
   requiring doors to balconies to be replaced by casements windows.

Wright was approached in 1938 by then college president Dr.
Ludd Spivey about designing "a great education temple in
Florida." His organic architecture, which did not dominate the
land but worked in harmony with it, can be seen here where his
structures "join" the rolling hills of orange groves.

   The hexagonal Annie Pfeiffer Chapel is the hallmark of the
Wright buildings on campus. Being a church-related college created certain expectations in the minds of parents and students.

The building of a chapel thus became the first concern in the Florida Southern College project. Student labor enabled this building to be constructed and the Chapel is considered to be a true specimen of Wright's work, with all the basic elements of his architecture integrated within. The larger plan is a hexagon, but the design is set on the six-foot square that informs all of Wright's Lakeland spaces. One can truly experience Wright's desire of being lifted "out of the ground, into the light and into the sun" while standing beneath the tower. The architect typically used colored pieces of glass to break the monotony of the blocks, allowing natural light to enter the auditorium from the side, while from above light falls through the mass of slanting skylights supported by a skeletal steel tower. The building's tower is known affectionately, among the students, staff, and local residents, as "the bicycle rack in the sky" and "the bow tie" because of the wrought iron work atop and the exterior concrete design respectively. The walls and structural members of the building are constructed of a buff-colored reinforced cast

Above left and right: William M. Holus Exhibition and Seminar Room.

Right: Interior of Florida Southern University.

concrete and, in keeping with Wright's ideas regarding ornament as integral to the structure, is the contrast of smooth and textured surfaces.

Wright's master plan for the campus called for eighteen buildings using the following basic materials: "steel for strength; sand because it was native to Florida; and glass to bring God's outdoors into man's indoors." Twelve structures were built with six left on the drawing board. Esplanades—necessary to shelter students from, on the one hand, tropical downpours and, on the other, a fierce summer sun—were built in 1946 to link all Wright's buildings on the campus. Florida Southern College, the "Child of the Sun" collection, is the largest-one-site-collection in the world. Wright described the pattern of the West Campus as "the cultural value of organic buildings well suited to time, purpose, and place."(*Architectural Forum*, January 1948)

Taliesin West

11000 Shea Road, Scottsdale, Arizona

Including the main unit, Wright's quarters and office, the
 drafting studio, kitchen and dining room, apprentices'
 quarters.
Sun Trap (1937). Sun Cottage (1948), remodeling of Sun
 Trap (1937). Cabaret Theatre (1949).
Constantly altered over the years as Wright's and the
 Fellowship's needs changed.
Open to the public. Tours available.

Wright's winter home for the Taliesin Fellowship is a complex of
buildings that includes a theater, music pavilion, and Sun
Cottage and offered a new challenge in building materials.
 In 1934, Wright bought 600 acres of rugged and dry land in
the Sonoran Desert at the foot of the McDowell Mountains and

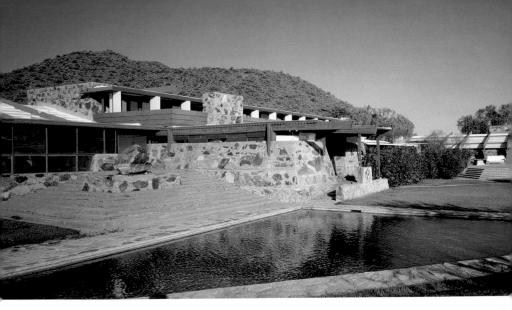

established an experimental "camp" that would serve as his winter home, studio, and "laboratory" of architectural ideas for the next twenty-two years. Taliesin West was the name Wright finally gave this winter home for the Taliesin Fellowship on Maricopa Mesa after others, including "Taliesin in the Desert" failed.

He first started work on the site with apprentices from Taliesin North. Over the years the complex was gradually altered and expanded to include a drafting room, offices and studios, private living quarters, no fewer than three theaters, and a workshop, as well as accommodation for the fellows and staff. For the first two years of construction they all lived in the desert in tents or temporary wood and canvas shelters. Life was primitive with no water, electricity, heating, or plumbing.

Above , below, and left: Wright's winter home, studio, and architectural laboratory known as Taliesin West in Scottsdale, Arizona.

It was partly built using what Wright described as "desert rubblestone wall" (usually shortened to "desert masonry"), a construction which involved large stones set in concrete, to produce a more colorful and natural effect than pure concrete. The mortar was allowed to seep around the edges of the stone face, and the surplus was then chipped away to reveal the stone surface. The structures seemed to grow naturally out of the desert as the textures and colors of the building materials blended with the landscape. The forms and materials of the exterior walls are also evident indoors where the masonry and exposed beams are both structural and decorative.

Influenced by the wooden structure erected for the Ocatillo Desert Camp, Wright built much of Taliesin West from linen canvas on redwood frames, which diffused the harsh desert sun—today fiberglass and steel have replaced much of this. They started with tents which was followed by a wood and linen structure that later gained a full concrete slab floor and a

Below and right: Interior views of Taliesin West.

hearth when Taliesin West was truly born, in the form of Sun Trap. Eventually, Sun Trap was transformed into a truly permanent structure, Sun Cottage.

The living room at Taliesin West is dominated by the rugged masonry hearth and is framed by redwood forms that support the ceiling panels. The triangular motif of the windows and hearth reflect the shape of the surrounding mountains. At the heart of the complex is the ninety-six-foot by thirty-six-foot drafting room, a communal dining room, and two apartments. A terrace links these "core" spaces and leads to a fifty-six-foot-long garden room with a sloping, translucent roof.

Taliesin West has been designated by the AIA as one of seventeen examples of Wright's architectural contribution to American culture that must be kept unspoiled. Taliesin West now houses the Taliesin Fellowship for much of the year as well as staff for the Frank Lloyd Wright Memorial Foundation.

1939

In the spring of 1939, Wright was extremely busy with some of his most ambitious projects. The administration building for S. C. Johnson & Son Co. opened, "Fallingwater" was completed, plans were well under way for the campus of Florida Southern College in Lakeland, and the Community Church in Kansas City, Missouri, was about to break new ground. Wright was invited to London to give a series of lectures by the Royal Institute of British Architects. Two years later he was presented with the Royal Gold Medal for Architecture by that same august body. Wright also addressed the Arts and Crafts Society where forty years earlier he had given his famous lecture—"The Art and Craft of the Machine."

1939 BUILDINGS

Andrew F. Armstrong House,
Ogden Dunes, Indiana.

Crystal Heights Hotel,
Washington DC.

Goetsch-Winkler House I,
Okemos, Michigan.

Stanley Rosenbaum House,
Florence, Alabama.

Bernard Schwartz House,
Two Rivers, Wisconsin.
(*Left.*)

George D. Sturges House
"Skyeway", Brentwood
Heights, California.

Suntop Homes (quadruple
house), Ardmore,
Pennsylvania.

Frank Lloyd Wright writings & publications

An Organic Architecture: The Architecture of Democracy (transcript of four lectures given at the Royal Institute of British Architects in London), published by Lund Humphries.

To The Fifty-Eighth published by the *Journal of the Royal Institute of British Architects* (October).
This is a rebuttal to the criticisms brought about by his London lectures in 1939. He also confronted the proponents of the International Style, "I suggest you put a gently sloping roof on any Le Corbusier or Gropius (building) just to see what you have left of the so-called International Style after proper deductions have been made."

Dinner talk at Hull House: November 8

Almost forty years after his first talk given at Chicago's Hull House, founded as a social settlement by Jane Addams in 1889, Wright was invited to return to deliver another lecture. He reiterated some of the points he had made in the 1901 Paper *The Art and Craft of the Machine* but this time spoke of how the machine had indeed taken over the twentieth century.

PROJECTS

Bell House, Los Angeles, California. The project was built in 1974 as the Feldman House (designed in 1939, built in 1974), 13 Mosswood Road, Berkeley, California. Built long after Wright's death, this Usonian House required 30,000 bricks. California clearheart redwood is used in the trim and for the board and batten walls. The original design was for the Lewis N. Bell House, intended for a west Los Angeles placement.

Carlson House, Superior, Wisconsin.

Crystal Heights Hotel, Shops, and Theaters, Washington DC.

Front gates for Taliesin, Spring Green, Wisconsin.

Mauer House, Los Angeles, California.

Spivey House, Fort Lauderdale, Florida.

Usonian House Development (seven buildings), Okemos, Michigan.

Left: Goetsch-Winkler House

Stanley & Mildred Rosenbaum Residence

117 Riverview Drive, Florence, Alabama

Addition (1948)
Open to the public, guided tours available by appointment.

This is the only example of Wright's work in Alabama and the design is an elaboration of the basic Usonian L-plan. Beyond the masonry, which supports the extensive cantilevering, at the far end of the living room is a study with its own fireplace. Turned parallel to the wing axis, the masonry for cantilever support at the end of the bedroom wing is practically invisible. The living area built-in furniture was specially designed by Wright and made from cypress wood. Wright extends the basic plan, with a second bathroom exclusively for the master bedroom.

Above right: Bathroom.

Below right: Living room.

Below: The design is based on a basic Usonian L-plan.

The architect himself enlarged the house in 1948 when he extended the structure opposite the living room, creating a dormitory for the Rosenbaum's sons. A separate gallery, parallel to the original one, was then added to lead to a guest bedroom. The three new spaces framed a lanai that was subsequently converted into a Japanese garden. The house was completely renovated in 1970 by the Taliesin Associated Architects.

George D. Sturges House, "Skyeway"

449 Skyeway Drive, Brentwood Heights, Los Angeles, California

Alarmingly cantilevered out from its hillside site in Brentwood
Heights, the whole east side of the house opens out onto a balcony overlooking the street below and presents the impression
of a house without windows. The building is constructed from
brick and painted redwood siding, and the solidity of the brickwork on the entrance side of the building contrasts with the
sense of lightness of the deck, balustrade, and row of glass
doors on the street side. The balcony-terrace is nine six-foot-six-
inch-square units long, four for the living room, two each for
the bedrooms and one for the side terrace. Workspace, utilities,
and the bathroom are behind the bedrooms on the opposite
side of the gallery. For such a limited interior space (less than
900 square feet), Wright cleverly made it seem more spacious by

*Right: The house opens up to a
balcony overlooking the street.*

*Below: "Skyeway" gives the
impression of a house without
windows.*

intimately relating the outside to the interior by way of the terrace.

Wright's preferred heart redwood, a reasonable substitute for cypress—not readily available on the West Coast—proved to be too soft over time. A later owner of the house began replacing the wood, which had begun to rot, as the house entered its fifth decade.

Left: The terrace makes the interior seem more spacious.

Below: The hearth.

1940

Between 1940 and 1942, with U.S. involvement in the war in Europe a looming threat, Wright became a vocal opponent of participation. He aired his pacifist views in ten essays, the most notorious of which was entitled *Wake up America!* (published in *Christian Century* in November 1940). Wright's antiwar stance and his open sympathy for the Japanese, which he still promoted even after their attack on Pearl Harbor, gathered more enemies to go with his already considerable collection. He fell out with a number of his friends including his once close friend Lewis Mumford, who would eventually lose his only son in the war, and even his cousin Richard Lloyd Jones—"Hell Frank, if you don't like the system on which this country's run, why don't you get out of it? Go somewhere else! God-dammit."

The year marked the founding of The Frank Lloyd Wright Foundation, a non-profit making corporation with tax exemption incorporated in the State of Wisconsin. To this foundation

1940 BUILDINGS

Gregor S. Affleck House,
   Bloomfield Hills, Michigan.
   (*Left and inset.*)

Auldbrass, Stevens
   Plantation, Yemassee,
   South Carolina.

Theodore Baird House,
   Amherst, Massachusetts.

Sidney Bazett House,
   Hillsborough, California.
   (*Overleaf.*)

James B. Christie House,
   Bernardsville, New Jersey.

Joseph Euchtman House,
   Baltimore, Maryland.

Wright gave his work, his homes, his property, and the art collections he acquired after 1940. In this way he made certain that his work as well as his intellectual property would be protected into the future.

Frank Lloyd Wright writings & publications

Wake up America!, published in *Christian Century* (November). The following inflammatory declaration from this essay caused a mighty furore and turned many people against Wright:

"During several months past I could 'listen in' or read at any time anywhere and imagine myself back in the stupid days of 1914. But that previous catastrophe to the economy and morale of our democratic world was nothing compared to what now takes us in its grip. Shame enough to sell out our best thought at first sign of danger and see our nationals run pell-mell to play a second-hand imitation of the enemy when our power can never lie in saving empire unless we too are empirical. Imitation always base, never yet won a battle. No, our real enemy is not Hitler! Our real enemy lies in our own timidity and stupidity as seen in this frightful current so smoothly moved, coaxed in the

1940 BUILDINGS CONTINUED

Kansas City Community
   Christian Church. (Overleaf,
   right and inset.)

Lloyd Lewis House,
   Libertyville, Illinois.

Charles L. Manson House,
   Wausau, Wisconsin.
   (*Overleaf, top left*)

Rose Pauson House, Phoenix,
   Arizona.

John C. Pew House,
   Shorewood Hills,
   Wisconsin.

Pope-Leighey House,
   Woodlawn, Virginia.

Clarence Sondern House,
   Kansas City, Missouri.

*Left and inset: Sidney Bazett
House*

direction of self-destruction. 'To save Britain?' No, to maintain Britain as our only shield against our own slavery or destruction is the insane notion sold to mediocrity by way of its own sales-men, from chief executive to the journalistic horde."

To Arizona, published in *Arizona Highways* (May). It included the first published photographs of Taliesin West.

Chicago's Auditorium is Fifty Years Old, published in the *Architectural Forum* (September) on the fiftieth anniversary of the completion of Adler & Sullivan's great building.

The New Frontier: Broadacre City, published in *Taliesin Magazine* (October).
All the various texts and articles on Broadacre City were com-piled together in this publication.
"Broadacre City represented a definite solution that can even now be observed if life—one worth living—is to survive on this planet. Many ideas first instigated . . . have indeed already become part of our daily life, among them the shopping center accessed by the automobile, the highway motel, and the general trend toward decentralization."

PROJECTS

Model House (exhibition project) Museum of Modern Art, New York.

Nesbitt House, Carmel Bay, California.

Oboler House "Eaglefeather," Los Angeles, California.

Pence House, Hilo, Hawaii.

Rentz House, Madison, Wisconsin.

Watkins Studio, Barnegate City, New Jersey.

Methodist Church, Spring Green, Wisconsin.

Left and above: Kansas City Community Christian Church
Far Left: Charles L. Manson House

Pope-Leighey House

Woodlawn Plantation, 9000 Richmond Highway, Mount Vernon, Virginia

Open March to December.

This house is an outstanding example of the Usonian idea seen at its simplest and most functionally effective. Wright designed this 1,200-square-foot house—an L-plan structure on a two-by-four foot rectangular unit—for Washington journalist Loren Pope and his wife for a cost of $7,000. The building is a typical horizontal sunk cypress batten dry-wall construction around a brick core. Typical of other Usonian designs, the Pope-Leighey House is modest in scale, has a flat roof with cantilevered carport, a heated concrete floor slab, recessed lighting, and uniform treatment of exterior and interior walls.

When, in 1963, the Virginia State Highway Commission earmarked the house for demolition, its second owner, Mrs. Robert

Leighey, donated the building to the National Trust for Historic Preservation and Mrs. Leighey was offered a life tenancy. The Trust disassembled it in its entirety and moved it fifteen miles from its site in Falls Church to a similar wooded hilltop location on the Woodlawn Plantation. During its relocation process, the house was improperly oriented to the sun and many details of design and construction were ignored. Foundation and heating pipes were cracked during the reconstruction.

Above, left and right: Interior of Pope-Leighey House showing clerestory panels.

1941

The USA is drawn into the Second World War with the Japanese attack on Pearl Harbor.

In 1941 an anthology of Wright's writings, *Frank Lloyd on Architecture*, was published.

From 13 November 1940 to 4 January 1941, The Museum of Modern Art in New York held the largest exhibition to date of Wright's work: "Frank Lloyd Wright: American Architect."

Frank Lloyd Wright writings & publications

The first of the *Taliesin Square-Papers*, which served as a vehicle for Wright to voice his views and make them public, was published. There were seventeen papers in all published from January 1941 to February 1953.

Taliesin Square-Paper Number 2 (May)
Of all Wright's anti-interventionist essays, the most prophetic by far was this piece entitled *Of What Use Is a Great Navy with No Place to Hide?* This essay uncannily foresaw the Japanese destruction of the Americans at Pearl Harbor on December 7, 1941.

Taliesin Square-Paper Number 3: Good Afternoon, Editor Evjue (June)

Taliesin Square-Paper Numbers 4: Defense & 5: To Beat the Enemy (July)

Taliesin Square-Paper Number 6: Usonia, Usonia South, and New England (August)

Mumford Lectures, published in *The Saturday Review* (August).
This was Wright's attack on Lewis Mumford for a series of lectures he gave on *The South in Architecture*. In fact Wright's intense disagreements with Mumford were really a result of their differing views about the United States entering the war in Europe.

1941 BUILDINGS

Oboler Gatehouse and Retreat, Malibu, California.

Stuart Richardson House, Glen Ridge, New Jersey (Richardson Co. of Milwaukee, American Systems Bungalow). (*Left.*)

Carlton D. Wall House, "Snowflake," Plymouth, Michigan.

PROJECTS
Barton House, Pine Bluff, Wisconsin.

Dayer Music Studio, Detroit, Michigan.

Ellinwood House, Deerfield, Illinois.

Field House, Peru, Illinois.

Guenther House, "Mountain Lakes", East Caldwell, New Jersey.

Petersen House, West Racine, Wisconsin.

Schevill House, Tuscon, Arizona.

Sigma Chi Fraternity House, Hanover, Indiana.

Sundt House, Madison, Wisconsin.

Waterstreet Studio, Spring Green, Wisconsin.

Stuart Richardson Residence

Glen Ridge, New Jersey

Kitchen remodeled. Accordion-pleated doors replaced by sliding doors.

This residence, for engineer Stuart Richardson, is most notable as an early example of Wright's use of triangular forms, while the plan of the living room is derived from a hexagonal concept. The unit module is a non-standard, twenty-eight-inch-sided hexagon. This Usonian dwelling is built primarily of masonry, with Wright's much-loved cypress used as trim more than as walls. Special brick with sixty- and 120-degree corners was made to fit the hexagonal unit. An unusual feature is the living room ceiling that slopes two feet, seven inches from the walls, just above the clerestory windows, down to the center point of the room.

In order to save on costs, many changes were made to the original design on site. The window doors to the shallow southeastern patio and western walled terrace were supposed to have been pivoted short of their centers. Instead they are standard wood frames held by full-length piano hinges. The since remodeled kitchen was originally installed to a design by the General Electric Home Bureau. Above deck lighting is used in the dining room with electric lighting sunk into the ceiling elsewhere in the dwelling.

1942

When the United States entered the Second World War, nineteen of Wright's apprentices were inducted into the armed services. Another was excused on the basis of his religious upbringing, and three others were sent to prison on the grounds of being conscientious objectors. When Marcus Weston, one of the conscientious objectors, was sentenced, twenty-five apprentices got together and signed a document—a plea—to the local draft board but the judge accused the apprentices of submitting a document that was seditious.

Frank Lloyd Wright's home life and personal circumstances
Wright, who had never received a commission from the U.S. government, was, however, presented with a federal job early in the year to design housing for defense plant workers in Pittsfield, Massachusetts. The scheme he proposed was a quadruple housing project based on the Suntop homes he had built in Ardmore, Pennsylvania, in 1939. Complete working drawings were prepared and signed and work was about to begin but was suddenly halted. Wright stated that, although the people in Washington were generally delighted with his work, the local architects in Massachusetts had taken the matter up with their congressmen and that only local architects, as provided for in a statute covering the matter, would be allowed to handle the project.

1942 BUILDINGS

Circle Pines Resort, Cloverdale, Michigan.

PROJECTS
Burlingham House, El Paso, Texas (two versions of the planned house were built in the 1980s, one in Santa Fe, New Mexico, the second in Phoenix, Arizona).
Circle Pines Center, Cloverdale, Michigan.
Cloverleaf Quadruple Housing, Pittsfield, Massachusetts.
Cooperative Homesteads, Housing for Detroit Auto Workers, Michigan.

1943

In June, a letter came out of the blue from Baroness Rebay asking whether Wright would consider designing a new museum to contain Solomon R. Guggenheim's collection of non-objective paintings. Frank was immediately attracted by the prospect and signed a contract with Guggenheim on June 29, 1943. This was to be the start of a very enervating time for the architect. The museum had no site for nine months and Wright became increasingly disgruntled with the project. New York and its bureaucracy, its planning authorities, in particular the Commissioner Robert Moses, became the bane of his life. Intellectually their minds had no meeting point: Moses had plans for New York which included building high-rise, high-density housing while Wright, in complete contrast, saw dispersed low-level homes as the only answer to housing the urban masses. A personal antipathy developed, in which Moses did all he could to obstruct the building of the museum.

The battle took sixteen years and when Guggenheim died in November 1949, the project was in jeopardy for a time until his bequest was sorted out.

Frank Lloyd Wright's home life and personal circumstances

Work in the studio had again slowed down due to the war effort. Conscription had taken nineteen apprentices into the armed services, and those who remained had received farm deferments. Because of this lull in architectural work Wright once again turned to writing, "We have shut down Hillside for the winter and with the big root cellar filled, what is there left of us except to come forth in the spring with double chins—As for me I am a 'writer' now."

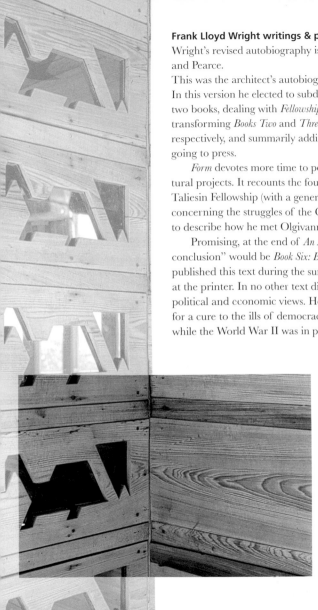

Frank Lloyd Wright writings & publications

Wright's revised autobiography is published by Quell, Sloan, and Pearce.

This was the architect's autobiography published in its entirety. In this version he elected to subdivide the original *Book One* into two books, dealing with *Fellowship* and *Family* separately, thereby transforming *Books Two* and *Three* into *Books Three* and *Four*, respectively, and summarily adding a fifth book, *Form*, before going to press.

Form devotes more time to personal events than to architectural projects. It recounts the founding and the early years of the Taliesin Fellowship (with a generous portion of the narrative concerning the struggles of the Great Depression) and goes on to describe how he met Olgivanna.

Promising, at the end of *An Autobiography*, that the "natural conclusion" would be *Book Six: Broadacre City*, Wright privately published this text during the summer while *An Autobiography* was at the printer. In no other text did Wright more clearly define his political and economic views. He concluded with his suggestions for a cure to the ills of democracy as he saw them in 1943, even while the World War II was in progress.

1944

At this time the battle to build the Guggenheim Museum almost completely took over Wright. The cost of the project naturally escalated and accordingly the plans were revised time and again to reduce the expense as much as possible. In total Wright drew up eight complete sets of plans (the first set contained twenty-nine architectural drawings and thirteen structural drawings). Guggenheim believed that building costs would drop in time so he postponed the project, but things just got more expensive.

On March 13, the property between 88th and 89th streets was obtained for the project.

Frank Lloyd Wright writings & publications

How Shall We Rebuild Our Cities in the *AIA Journal*, April. Although no bombs had fallen on American cities, many of them had suffered for years from overcrowding, from blighted areas and slums, and from antiquated housing facilities. Wright's thoughts on these issues were, expectedly, based on his idea of decentralisation, "spared the bomb—how to proceed? Decentralization is our true answer."

Taliesin Square-Paper Number 7: To The Mole (August)
When Wright proposed his Broadacre City plan to his cousin Robert Moses, parks commissioner of the City of New York, Moses responded with an article in the *New York Times Magazine* entitled *Mr Moses Dissects the "Long Haired Planners": The Park Commissioner Prefers Common Sense to Their Revolutionary Theories*. The *Taliesin Square Paper Number 7* was Wright's counter response to Moses. He concludes his article with,
"You can't expect anything better from moles who are blind, crawl short distances under the earth, and have only the most limited objectives."

1944 BUILDINGS

S. C. Johnson Wax Company Research Tower, Racine, Wisconsin. (*Right.*)

PROJECTS

Loeb House (Pergola House), Redding, Connecticut.
Harlan House, Omaha, Nebraska.
Wells House, Minneapolis, Minnesota.

S. C. Johnson Co. Research Tower

1525 Howe Street, Racine, Wisconsin.

Heliolaboratory for Herbert F. Johnson, Jr., president,
Johnson Wax Company.
Free tours conducted during business hours.

The Research Tower is a more conventional building than the
Administration Building (see 1936), yet has still become a significant landmark. Using a circular yet rectilinear theme, the
Research Tower echoes the central support principles of the
dendriform columns of the Administration Building. The floors
of the fourteen-story tower are cantilevered out from a central
core that contains the stairwell, elevator shafts, and the electrical and mechanical systems. The cantilevered concrete slabs
form alternating square floors and circular balconies contained
in a skin of brick and glass and the whole tower is linked to the
main building by a covered bridge. At the base of the tower are
pools and sculptures—additions made after Wright's death by
the Taliesin Associated Architects. The additional stories to the
east of the tower, based on Wright's plans, were constructed in
1961. In 1978 two black granite sculptures representing the figures of Nakoma and Nakomis, which Wright had designed in
1924 for an unexecuted project, were installed in the Research
Tower courtyard.

With his design of the Research Tower, Wright demonstrat-
ed that he was no longer confined to horizontal structures and
brought the geometric form of the circle into his architecture.

The Administration Building and the Tower are generally
recognized as two of the most remarkable structures of their
time and have been designated by the AIA as two of the seventeen buildings designed by Wright to be retained as supreme
examples of his architectural contribution to American culture.

1945

The war years halted most construction in America and only three of Wright's 1941 designs were built and none from 1942. From his 1943 efforts, the Guggenheim design had to wait nearly a decade before the foundation was laid. In 1945 construction activity resumed.

The first set of working drawings for the museum was finished and signed by Wright on September 7, and countersigned by Solomon R. Guggenheim as proof of his approval of the scheme.

Frank Lloyd Wright writings & publications
When Democracy Builds, University of Chicago Press, 1945.

Taliesin Square-Paper Number 8: The Price of Peace (May)
This article expresses Wright's reaction to the San Francisco Peace Conference at which the United Nations charter was drawn up. "We are coming in sight of a ghastly War wherein four-fifths of the population of the Earth—(yellow)—will be solidly lined up in hatred with murderous resentment (justified) against attempted domination by one fifth—(white)!" Wright correctly predicted that the UN would act more as a police force than as a peaceful assembly of nations.

Taliesin Square-Paper Number 9: Nature (August)
Wright continues the thesis he began in *The Price of Peace* and, in the unconditional surrender documents, he saw old mistakes and misconceptions about "peace" continuing:

"We should realize that peace has never been won and never can be won by violence. We should know that constant resource and continual reference to the principles of Nature in order to make them manifest to men is the only education—the only safe way to take with any attempt at civilization."

1945 BUILDINGS

Arnold Friedman House, "The Fir Tree," Pecos, New Mexico.

Lowell Walter House and River Pavilion, Quasqueton, Iowa. (*Left.*)

PROJECTS

Adelman Laundry, Milwaukee, Wisconsin.

Berdan House, Ludington, Michigan.

Elizabeth Arden Desert Spa, Phoenix, Arizona.

"Glass House" project for *Ladies' Home Journal*.

Haldorn House "The Wave," Carmel, California.

Slater House, Rhode Island.

Stamm House, Lake Delavan, Wisconsin.

Lowell and Agnes Walter Residence

2611 Quasqueton Diag. Boulevard, Quasqueton, Iowa

Council Fire and gate.

River Pavilion (1948) restored in 1991 with a complete
rebuilding of several walls.

The Walter House and River Pavilion are public property,
having been given by the Walters to the people of
Iowa upon Lowell's death in 1981. It is now known as
Cedar Rock Park and is open to the public during the
summer months.

The eleven-acre site Cedar Rock is part of a limestone bluff on
the left bank of the Wapsipinicon River. Although the basic
design for Walter House was completed by 1945, construction
could not begin until 1948 because of wartime limitations on
building materials. The main house, which Wright called his

"Opus 497"—roughly the number of designs Wright reckoned he had produced by 1945—derives from the "glass house" for the *Ladies' Home Journal*. It is a Usonian L-plan brick and steel construction with a reinforced concrete roof, pierced as a trellis in its overhang, with steel, glass, walnut, and brick elsewhere. The roof, with its broad overhanging eaves, is designed to support a rooftop garden. Inside the house the board and batten walls are executed in walnut and all the furnishings were carried out to Wright's designs.

The original plan, on a completely regular square module, sixty-three inches to the side, has three bedrooms, and the 900 square-foot living room is given focus by a fireplace. The combined living room, dining alcove, conservatory, and three exterior glass walls, referred to here as a "garden room," is turned thirty degrees to afford dramatic views of the river. The interior garden of the conservatory area is provided with natural light by a central clerestory and skylight.

As in most Usonian designs the heating employs a gravity system but the half-unit slabs set directly on the aggregate in which the heating pipes are laid are unique to this house. Also unique is the Pullman-type combination of sink, toilet, and bathtub used for the bathrooms in the main house and the maid's quarters.

The materials used for the River Pavilion, with its boathouse below and sun terrace above, are the same as in the main residence but it is more screened than glazed. This structure, further down the river than the main residence, also has a reinforced concrete roof imitating that of the house, though with less trellising. The boathouse was designed to withstand river flooding, while the upper-level sun terrace is above the highest-known water level. On a knoll above the main house stands the Council Fire, an area enclosed by a low semi-circular wall around an old outdoor hearth.

1946

Frank Lloyd Wright's home life and personal circumstances

Tragedy struck the Wrights in the autumn when their daughter Svetlana was killed in an automobile accident. Svetlana was Olgivanna's daughter by a previous marriage, and was married to one of Frank's favorite apprentice's, William Wesley Peters.

Frank Lloyd Wright writings & publications

The Modern Gallery, published in the *Magazine of Art* (January)
This text explained the Guggenheim Museum building. At this point in time, neither the architect nor his client could possibly foresee the myriad difficulties that would go on for another decade and which was to prove the most arduous and painful commission of Wright's entire career.

Why I Believe in Advancing Unitarianism, published by the American Unitarian Association (May).
In this essay Wright extols the Unitarian faith and emphasizes the resources needed for the Atomic Era and Organic Architecture.

Starched Churches—Review of the Church Beautiful, published in the *Christian Register* (August).

Taliesin Square-Paper 10: Building a Democracy (October) "A democratic building is at ease, it stands relaxed. A democratic building, again, is for and belongs to the people. It is of human scale, for men and women to live in and feel at home."

1946 BUILDINGS

Douglas Grant House, Cedar Rapids, Iowa.

Chauncey L. Griggs House, Tacoma, Washington.

Alvin Miller House, Charles City, Iowa.

Melvin Maxwell Smith House, Bloomfield Hills, Michigan.

PROJECTS

President's House, Olivet College, Michigan.
Dayer House and Music Pavilion, Bloomfield Hills, Michigan.
Garrison House, Lansing, Michigan.
Hause House, Lansing, Michigan.
Housing for State Teacher's College, Lansing, Michigan.
Morris House I, San Francisco, California.
Munroe House, Knox County, Ohio.
Newman House, Lansing, Michigan.
Oboler Studio, Los Angeles, California.
Panshin House, State Teacher's College, Lansing, Michigan.
Pinderton House, Cambridge, Massachusetts.
Pinkerton House, Fairfax County, Virginia.
Rogers Lacy Hotel, Dallas, Texas.
Sarabhi Administration Building and Store, Ahmedabad, India.
Van Dusen House, Lansing, Michigan.

Chauncey and Johanna Griggs Residence

7800 John Dower S.W., Tacoma, Washington

The roofing and sidings of the Griggs House, located at the foot of a hill on Chambers Creek, are of cedar planks laid diagonally and horizontally giving the house the impression of a log cabin —in fact logs had originally been considered.

The house features a two-story facade on the inside of its basic L-plan and the deeply recessed glass wall opens the gallery, at the end of which is space for a formal dining room, to the yard. The gallery wing has glazing just below the eaves. At the top of the L is the master bedroom while at the bottom end a lounge, large enough for the performance of chamber music, is separated from the workspace and dining room by the masonry core.

The concrete slab floor, scored to mark the unusual seven-foot-square unit module, was laid long before the concrete-block was raised. This delay was due to soaring post-war construction costs and the fact that good stone was not available.

This charming house displays a rustic simplicity without sacrificing the amenities that usually disappear in such a structure.

1947

In 1947 the National Institute of Art and Letters made Wright a member and later presented him with the gold medal for architecture.

Frank Lloyd Wright writings & publications
The Architect was one of a series of lectures published in *The Works of the Mind*, University of Chicago Press.
This essay constitutes one of Wright's finest descriptions of the architect's obligations to society, "I think Organic Architecture should begin in the American home . . . this is where the ideal of something integral, something of life and not on it, something with which you can live with grave and intimate considerations of the things more excellent —and a feeling that you are some-body in your own right; feel like somebody yourselves because there is a harmony in the atmosphere of things you have created about you."

We Must Shape True Inspiration, published in the *New York Times* on April 20.
This article contained Wright's comments about the proposed headquarters in New York City for the recently founded United Nations. The thought of housing the UN in a skyscraper seemed totally inappropriate to him, "The city skyscraper is exploitation, therefore abuse of principle . . . a sinister emblem for world power." Wright advocated a scheme that would place the building out on the landscape, "where nature speaks and the beauty of organic order shows more clearly the true pattern of all peace whatsoever."

1947 BUILDINGS

Amy Alpaugh House, Northport, Michigan.

A. H. Bulbulian House, Rochester, Minnesota.

Jack Lamberson House, Oskaloosa, Iowa.

Unitarian Meeting House, Shorewood Hills, Wisconsin. (*Right.*)

Usonia Homes, Pleasantville, New York.

Planning Man's Physical Environment, published in the *Journal of Modern Culture* in California (March). Before proposing a plan for "man's physical environment," Wright, in this article, addresses some of the problems facing the United States and its society before going on to propose the panacea:

"The remedy is more Freedom . . . greater growth of Individuality—more men developed by the way of self-discipline from within the man . . . Under the watchful care of the people themselves, government must take its place down under, not up above the right of the individual to be himself."

Right: Unitarian Meeting House

PROJECTS

Wetmore Auto Display Room and
  Workshop, Detroit, Michigan.
Bell House, East St. Louis, Illinois.
Black House, Rochester, Minnesota.
Boomer House, Phoenix, Arizona.
Butterfly Bridge over the Wisconsin
  River, Spring Green, Wisconsin.
Cottage Group Resort Hotel, Los
  Angeles, California.
San Antonio Transit Company Depot,
  San Antonio, Texas.
Daphne Funeral Chapels, San
  Francisco, California.
Hamilton House, Brookline, Vermont.
Hartford House, Hollywood, California.
Houston House, Schuyler County,
  Illinois.
Keith House, Oakland County,
  Michigan.
Marting House, Northampton, Ohio.
Palmer House, Phoenix, Arizona.
Pike House, Los Angles, California.
Ayn Rand House, near Redding,
  Connecticut.
Sports Club, Hollywood, California.
Wheeler House, Hinsdale, Illinois.
Wilkie House, Hennepin County,
  Minnesota.
Valley National Bank, Tuscon, Arizona.

Unitarian Meeting House

900 University Bay Drive, Shorewood Hills, Wisconsin

Education wing added by Taliesin Associated Architects.
Open for visits weekdays and Saturdays, as well as for
Sunday worship. Guided tours available during sum-
mer months. The building is closed during mid-August.

Wright's parents were among the earliest members of the
Unitarian Society when it was organized in 1879, and the architect himself had a long history of association with the
movement. It was, therefore, no great surprise that he accepted
the commission to design a new church for the Unitarians.
Wright described the limestone and oak structure as a hilltop
"country church." Most of the labor came from the volunteer
workforce of the congregation itself who carted more than
1,000 tons of rough-cut limestone from a quarry thirty miles
away.

The original building covered approximately 11,500 square
feet and the module employed is the "diamond," an equilateral
parallelogram with a unit side of four feet scored into the concrete floor. This diamond shape is repeated in the largest forms
of the building—the main 252-seater auditorium with hearth
room behind—as well as the smaller elements such as the stone
piers. Wright designed the single and double benches in a way
that they could be removed for concerts.

The auditorium is triangular in plan, with the minister at the
apex and small choir loft above and behind. It is designed to
face the rising sun. The hearth room, differentiated from the
auditorium by an overhanging low ceiling, which it shares with
the entrance lobby, can be employed to enlarge the auditorium
space as required. A bronze tablet to the right of the hearth
room's fireplace (taken from the Society's first building) pro-
claims the Bond of Union—the statement of principle of the
First Unitarian Society of Madison. On the face of the low ceiling

over the hearth room is an ancient parable dictated by Wright: "Do you have a loaf of bread, break the loaf in two and give half for some flowers of the Narcissus for thy bread feeds the body indeed but the flowers feed the soul."

The green copper roof of the church, which rises from the hearth room to a prow, is said to symbolize hands closed in prayer. The shape of the roof obviated the need for a separate steeple. A supplementary education wing, beyond the west living room, has been added by the Taliesin Associated Architects.

The church has been designated by the American Institute of Architects as one of the seventeen Frank Lloyd Wright buildings to be retained as an example of his architectural contribution to American culture.

Left and overleaf: Wright described the Unitarian Meeting House as a hilltop "country church."

1948

Frank Lloyd Wright writings & publications

To Howard, published in *Architectural Forum* (January).
This article was dedicated to Howard Myers, the editor of
Architectural Forum who had died in September 1947.

Taliesin Square-Paper Number 12: Harum – Scarum (May).
This article shows Wright's continuing attack on the worship of
the dollar. He perceived the current foreign policy as a sorry
spectacle and a vicious interference into the internal lives of
other nations. His cures were extreme and he concluded with a
program that he admitted threatened the "Almighty Dollar."

1948 BUILDINGS

Albert Adelman House, Fox Point, Wisconsin. (*Left, below and far left.*)

Caroll Alsop House, Oskaloosa, Iowa.

Erling Brauner House, Okemos, Michigan. (*Overleaf*)

Maynard P. Buehler House, Orinda, California. (*Page 369*)

Galesburg Country Homes:
Eric Pratt, Galesburg, Michigan.
David I Weisblatt House,
    Galesburg, Michigan.
Samuel Eppstein House,
    Galesburg, Michigan.

Herbert Jacobs House II (Solar Hemicycle), Middleton, Wisconsin.

V. C. Morris Gift Shop, San Francisco, California.

Lowell Walter River Pavilion.

Charles E. Weltzheimer House, Oberlin, Ohio.

Robert D. Winn House, Parkwyn Village, Kalamazoo, Michigan.

Left: Erling Brauner House

PROJECTS

Left: Maynard P. Buehler House

Herbert Jacobs House II

7033 Old Sauk Road, Middleton, Wisconsin

When the Jacobs' presented Wright with an exposed hilltop site swept by icy winds in winter, the architect wrote enthusiastically that they were to be made "the goats" for his latest experiment, a solar house. This is the first solar hemicycle based on circular segments, six degrees wide, of two stories, with its back set into the earth. It was protected from severe winter weather by this berm of earth yet, on the opposite side, there was a beautiful view. Its glassed private facade opens onto a sunken terrace four feet below floor level, so as to provide a pocket of air immediately in front of the windows and dead calm whatever the weather. Wright's term for his design was "streamlining," and is nowadays looked upon as an audacious early experiment in solar design.

In this structure, Wright eliminated the tunnel gallery by placing the bedrooms on a second level. The gallery is thereby transformed into a cantilevered balcony overlooking the two-story living room. This has the effect of unifying the interior

spaces in direct contrast to the Usonian structures with their separate living and "quiet" zones.

The upper level of the building is hung from steel ties, themselves suspended from one-by-twelve-inch boards, spanning from the north wall masonry to the south glazes-wall mullions.

Although the stone used in the construction of Jacobs' house is quite beautiful, the owner skimped on the lumber so that, even in the interior, it lacks the usual style and finesse associated with Wright houses of this period.

V. C. Morris Gift Shop

140 Maiden Lane, San Francisco, California

Open to the public during regular business hours.

This building employs innovative circular forms. With its brick facade, Romanesque splayed portal arch, and circular ramp, it is a Guggenheim in microcosm. The brick facade of the Morris building protects the internal contents as it invites visitors to enter the portal. Upstairs, a suspended glass screen of translucent circles framed in globes provided soft lighting for the fine crystal, glass, and porcelain, silver and gold objects on display.

Originally a gift shop, it has seen many owners and renovations and variously used as a dress shop and art gallery. In 1967 it became the Circle Gallery, housing contemporary paintings, sculpture, and jewelry. It has a stone floor with dark walnut trim and cabinetry.

The shop has been designated by the American Institute of Architects as one of the seventeen American buildings designed by Frank Lloyd Wright to be retained as an example of his architectural contribution to American culture.

1949

Although seventeen of Wright's buildings have been designated by the American Institute of Architects (AIA) as examples of his contribution to American culture, it was an institution he steadfastly refused to join. Wright referred to the institute as the "Arbitary Institute of Appearances." Often he maintained that the organization was founded to protect the members of the profession rather than to uphold the quality of architecture. On March 17, 1949, however, he was awarded the Gold Medal of the AIA and on accepting the award he acknowledged his gratitude to his colleagues: "Honors have reached me from almost every great nation in the world. Honor has, however, been a long time coming from home. But here it is at last. Handsomely, indeed. Yes . . . I am extremely grateful."

1949 BUILDINGS

Howard E. Anthony House, Benton Harbor, Michigan. (*Below.*)

James Edwards House, Okemos, Michigan.

Sol Friedman House, Usonia Homes, Pleasantville, New York.

In November 1949, Solomon Guggenheim died and the whole Guggenheim Museum project was put in jeopardy for a time until his bequest was sorted out.

Frank Lloyd Wright's home life and personal circumstances

In 1944, a group of friends formed the Rochdale Cooperative, later to become Usonia Homes, Inc., and went on to purchase ninety-seven acres of land in Pleasantville, within commuting distance north of New York City. Wright was engaged to design or approve the buildings to be constructed on this site. The site plan initially called for circular plots, an acre to each family, plus an acre for communal use. The circles were eventually adjusted to polygons to satisfy the Board of Assessors. The cooperative developed the overall site with water, electricity, and road systems as well as fire-fighting capabilities.

Above: Kenneth Laurent House

Frank Lloyd Wright writings & publications

Taliesin Square-Paper Number 13. This was Wright's AIA acceptance address for the Gold Medal he received.

Taliesin Square-Paper Number 14: We Want the Truth (November). This article continues to reveal Wright's sad disillusionment with what had transpired in the United States following the World War II. Yet, ever hopeful, he still professed great faith when he wrote, "To see things in their eternal significance is all that can ever really matter to us as true individuals and we must never forget that the individual free is the norm of Democracy."

Genius and the Mobocracy, Duell, Sloan and Pearce, 1949 (Enlarged edition, Secker and Warburg, 1972).
Wright's biography of, and tribute to, his old mentor Louis Sullivan who had died in poverty in 1924.

"Who then, was this Louis H. Sullivan I still call liebermeister so long after he is gone because he is still an inspiration to me? How did this 'pencil' come into his hand? This book is my attempt to answer. This book is 'in memoriam' because of a promise."

It is, however, far more than an account of the association between the two of them; it is also the study of the creative genius in a democratic society.

"Furthermore it is in the art of building wherein aesthetic and construction *not only approve and prove each other*. In organic sense such building is an entity of the human spirit as that of any tree or flower is of the ground. A natural, human circumstance—possible only to the complete architect. There will never be too many of them. He is the master of the elements: earth, air, fire, light, and water. Space, motion, and gravitation are his palette: the sun his brush. His concern is the heart of humanity. He, of all men, must see into the life of things; know their honor."

J. Willis Hughes House "Fountainhead", Jackson, Mississippi.

Kenneth Laurent House, Rockford, Illinois. (*Left.*)

Robert Levin House, Parkwyn Village, Kalamazoo, Michigan.

Ward McCartney House, Parkwyn Village, Kalamazoo, Michigan.

Herman T. Mossberg, South Bend, Indiana.

Edward Serlin House, Pleasantville, New York.

Left (above and below): Ward McCartney House.

Far left. Kenneth Laurent House.

Sol Friedman House

Usonia Homes, Pleasantville, New York

This was the first of the three houses built in Pleasantville's Usonia from Wright's designs. In terms of its geometry, it was also the most daring. The geometry is clearly marked in circular segments scored on the concrete floor mat. It is a two-story stone and concrete structure with oak trim, interlocking two cylinders, or drums, with a detached mushroom shaped carport that is reminiscent of the dendriform columns of the Johnson Wax Building of 1936. The workspace and utilities are on the main floor, in the smaller of the two cylinders, with the bedrooms above. A balcony overlooks the larger forty-four-foot outer cylinder that houses the living room.

Edward Serlin House

Pleasantville, New York

Additions to the east end by Aaron L. Resnick.

The Serlin House, the second of Wright's Pleasantville projects, employs stone, of mostly local origin, along with horizontal siding. In that siding, and the title "Usonia Homes," this represents a late effort by Wright in pure Usonian expression, with masonry to support cantilevers and inexpensive wood paneling between. The cypress siding is not configured as board and batten, but has a simple mitered edge to provide a V-groove at the join. Four fireplaces were incorporated into the structure.

1950

Harry S. Guggenheim was appointed president of the Guggenheim Foundation and supported Wright in his endeavors to get the museum built.

Still politically vocal, particularly with his antiwar views, Wright drew the attention of Senator McCarthy from his home state of Wisconsin, who tried to have him impeached as an anti-American communist.

1950 BUILDINGS

Robert Berger House, San Anselmo, California. (*Below.*)

Eric V. Brown House, Parkwyn Village, Kalamazoo, Michigan. (*Right: above and below.*)

John O. Carr House, Glenview, Illinois.

Raymond Carlson House, Phoenix, Arizona.

Currier Gallery of Art, Zimmerman House, Manchester, New Hampshire.

Richard Davis House, Marion, Indiana.

John A. Gillin House, Dallas, Texas.

Ina Harper House, St. Joseph, Michigan.

Thomas Keys House, Rochester, Minnesota.

Arthur C. Mathews House, Atherton, California. (*Opposite: above and below.*)

Curtis Meyer House, Galesburg Village, Kalamazoo, Michigan. (*Left and above.*)

Robert Muirhead House, Plato Center, Illinois.

Henry J. Neils House, Minneapolis, Minnesota.

William Palmer House, Ann Arbor, Michigan. (*Left and below.*)

Donald Schaberg House, Okemos, Michigan.

Seamour Shavin House, Chattanooga, Tennessee.

1950 BUILDINGS CONTINUED

Richard Smith House, Jefferson, Wisconsin.

J. A. Sweeton House, Cherry Hill, New Jersey.

David Wright House, Phoenix, Arizona.

PROJECTS
Achuff House, Wauwatosa, Wisconsin.
Auerbach House, Pleasantville, New York.
Carroll House, Wauwatosa, Wisconsin.
Chahroudi House I, Lake Mahopac, New York.
Conklin House, New Ulm, Minnesota.
Grover House, Syracuse, New York.
Hargrove House, Berkeley, California.

Jackson House, Madison, Wisconsin.
Jacobsen House, Montreal, Canada.
Montooth House, Rushville, Illinois.
Sabin House, Battle Creek, Michigan.
Leon Small House, West Orange, New Jersey.
Southwestern Christian Seminary, Phoenix,
    Arizona (Construction of First Christian Church
    began 1970 and completed 1972).
Stevens House, Park Ridge, Illinois.
Strong House, Kalamazoo, Michigan.
Wassel House, Philadelphia.

Above and right : Donald Schaberg House

Dr. Isadore Zimmerman Residence

Manchester, New Hampshire

Restored, and open to the public as a museum by arrangement with the Currier Gallery.

Wright called this house a "classic Usonian" and the Zimmermans responded by declaring that their home was "the most beautiful house in the world." The primary construction materials of this 1,667-square-foot house are red-glazed brick, upland Georgia trim, and flat terra-cotta tile for the roof. A solid masonry wall pierced by a high, continuous band of windows dominates the street facade while, in contrast, the garden facade is made of floor-to-ceiling glass, mitered at the corners.

The true dimensions of this building, designed to a four-foot-square unit module, are not apparent on approaching the house with the internal organization of space, variations in

Right: A quartet music stand forms part of the furniture in the living room.

Below: Zimmerman House exterior on the terrace side.

ceiling height, the use of built-in furniture, and the continuous concrete floor slab. Two bedrooms are clustered around the workspace, with its clerestory lighting, rather than stretched along the usual tunnel gallery.

Colorundum, a balanced formulation of non-slip aggregate, second only to diamond in hardness and "available in eleven decorator colors," was used in the concrete floor and was seen by Wright as the ideal solution to the uncarpeted areas of plain concrete.

Asphalt shingles replaced the original roofing and forced air heating was added when the original gravity system failed. Upon Mrs. Zimmerman's death in 1988—Dr. Zimmerman had died four years previously—the Currier Gallery of Art took possession of the building with an endowment from the Zimmerman estate.

Top: Exterior of the Zimmerman House showing the distincitive keyhole windows.

Above: The hearth is at the center of the living and dining area.

David Wright House

5212 East Exeter Road, Phoenix, Arizona

This was to be the home of David, Wright's fourth child, who was the contractor for the house. It is constructed from concrete blocks with a metal roof. The raised living spaces are reached by a spiral ramp, an important feature of many of Wright's designs. Wright also designed the furniture. Wright's son, David, was involved in promoting concrete block construction and his house in Phoenix is constructed of these materials. Because his father's plans were not consistent with concrete construction, a complete re-engineering of the project took place.

1951

In January a world-touring exhibition of Wright's work, entitled "Sixty Years of Living Architecture," opened in Philadelphia. In May, its European premiere opened to great acclaim in Florence. The exhibition showed his original drawings, architectural models, and huge photographs of many of his buildings and decorative objects.

1951 BUILDINGS

Benjamin Adelman House (Usonian Automatic), Phoenix, Arizona.

Charlcey Austin House, Greenville, South Carolina.

A. K. Chahroudi House II, Lake Mahopac, New York.

S. P. Elam House, Austin, Minnesota.

Below and right:
Charles F. Glore House.

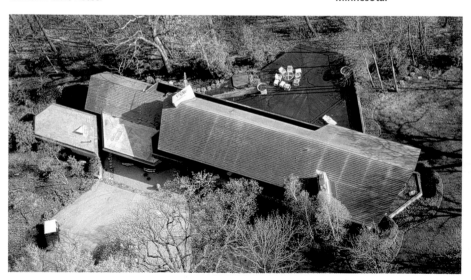

Price Company Tower

N.E. 6th Street at Dewey Avenue, Bartlesville, Oklahoma

Constructed for Harold C. Price. Guided tours available.

The Price Tower, a combined office and apartment block, is the only skyscraper Wright fully designed and gave him his one opportunity to make a major statement on what a skyscraper should be. The 186-foot tall tower is constructed with reinforced concrete, cantilevered floors, copper louvers, copper-faced parapets, and a gold-tinted glass exterior. The structure, based on the 1925 Saint Marks-in-the-Bouwerie, stands like a tall tree in the rolling hills of eastern Oklahoma, in Wright's words "dignified as a tree in the midst of nature, but a child of the spirit of man." The superstructure is like that of an evergreen tree, with a taproot holding a central trunk and the floors reaching out like branches. The building increases substantially in area from floor to floor as the tower rises, rather like the canopy of a tree.

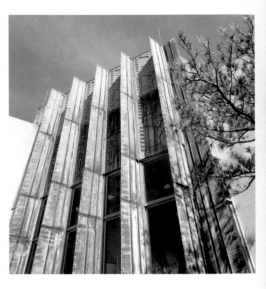

Above and right: The Price Company Tower is constructed with reinforced concrete and has gold-tinted glass on its exterior.

The building is planned on a two-foot six-inch equilateral parallelogram module and its nineteen floors are seventeen of tower and two of base, plus radio antenna spire. The tower's 37,000 square feet of interior floor space functioned as the corporate headquarters with additional space for apartments and offices. The larger plan of the tower shows a square overlaid on a pinwheel with the southwest quadrant, itself a rectangle, nestled into the pinwheel and containing eight two-story apartments. Toward the top of the tower the sixteenth floor has a buffet and kitchen with outside terraces, including planting

areas. The seventeenth floor has a small central office space with a Wright-signed mural, plus a living room that is at the top of the apartment. The nineteenth floor is not a complete quadrant, but contained Harold Price's own office. All the furnishings were custom designed for the building, including those for the apartments and for Price's own office.

This structure has been designated by the American Institute of Architects as one of the seventeen American buildings designed by Frank Lloyd Wright to be retained as an example of his architectural contribution to American culture. The building was purchased by the Philips Petroleum Company in 1981–82 and in 1983 won the American Institute of Architects 25 Year Award.

Left and below: The seventeenth and nineteenth floors have custom-built furniture and diamond-patterned murals.

Above and right: The furnishings were designed by Wright to unify the exterior and interior of the building.

Left: The top floor housed Price's office and had a rooftop garden overlooking the city.

1953

The world-touring exhibition of Wright's work, "Sixty Years of Living Architecture," arrived in New York and helped to keep up the momentum for the Guggenheim Museum project.

The house Wright designed for his son David, in Arizona, was put on exhibit at the National Institute of Art and Letters.

Frank Lloyd Wright writings & publications
The Future of Architecture, Horizon Press, 1953.
Organic architecture was, for Wright, "true" modern architecture. In this article he devised nine key words to clarify this:
• "Nature," which meant not just living things but was the essence of materials, plans, and feelings.

1953 BUILDINGS

Jorgine Boomer Cottage, Phoenix, Arizona.

Andrew Cooke Residence, Virginia Beach, Virginia. (*Above and left.*)

Lewis H. Goddard House, Plymouth, Michigan.

Louis Penfield House I, Willoughby Hills, Ohio.

Frank S. Sander House, Stamford, Connecticut.

Usonian Exhibition House, New York, New York.

Robert Llewellyn Wright House, Bethesda, Maryland.

- "Organic" referred to the relationship of parts to the whole.
- "Form and function" were one, unified.
- "Romance" was the creative force expressed by each individual embodied in the form of architecture.
- "Tradition" did not mean imitating the past, but implied a sense of belonging.
- "Ornament" was the emotional expression that was essential to, and should be integrated into, architecture, and which revealed and enhanced the structure of the building.
- "Spirit" was the essential life force within an object. The "Third Dimension" was the intrinsic depth of the building.
- "Space" was the "invisible fountain, from which all rhythm flows to which they must pass."

PROJECTS

Brewer House, East Fish, New York.

Lee House, Midland, Michigan.

Masieri Memorial Building, Grand Canal, Venice, Italy.

Morris House II ("Seacliff"), San Francisco, California.

Pieper and Montooth Office Building, Scottsdale, Arizona.

Pointview Residences Apartment Tower, Pittsburgh.

FM Radio Station, Jefferson, Wisconsin.

Rhodedendron Chapel, Bear Run, Pennsylvania.

Restaurant for Yosemite National Park, California.

Left: Andrew Cooke Residence

Robert Llewellyn Wright Residence

7927 Deepwell Drive, Bethesda, Maryland

This two-story concrete-block hemicycle, perched over a
ravine, was built for Wright's sixth child, Robert
Llewellyn Wright.

When the Wrights bought this site on a steep wooded slope it
was quite perfect from Frank Lloyd Wright's point of view, since
by then all his experimental work was encompassing circular
forms. He designed a two-story hemicycle made from concrete
block and specially curved boards of Philippine mahogany, with
plenty of extra mahogany used for interior detailing. It is wood-
faced at the second story where a stunning balcony, coming off
the master bedroom, continues the hemicircular line. It has a
cantilevered porch, and a southwest-facing terrace and pool.

    The standard practice of placing the interior surface of exte-
rior masonry on the grid line is observed here but the unit
system for a hemicycle created unique dimensional problems.
Usually, Wright specified an angular dimension in some multiple
of fifteen degrees, occasionally half that, but here
the grid lines are at 6.9 degrees. The unit is six
feet, or four and a half concrete blocks, on the
line at the radius for the wall that is the public
facade. This seventy-two-inch unit is also twice
the spacing between the radius lines. In this
house, air heat is used throughout the building.
Usually, in such a two-story house, gravity heat
was used downstairs and baseboard heat upstairs.

    Robert and his wife, Betty, loved the whole
concept of this house but regretted, in retrospect,
that they had scaled down some aspects of the
original design because, as they also observed,
the house was, for all practical purposes, impossible to enlarge.

*Overleaf: Mahogany is used for
the interior detailing, echoing the
curved boards of he exterior.*

*Left and below: The Wright House
is a circular form set on a wooded
slope.*

1954

For the duration of his work on the Guggenheim Museum, and his other projects in New York and Connecticut, Wright moved to New York where his favorite place to stay was the Plaza Hotel, within which he had remodeled a three-room apartment suite and had it refurbished to his specifications. He had always worked where he ate and slept and this was no exception, one room was part office and reception. As usual, he surrounded himself with expensive luxury and installed sleek black lacquer tables, a golden peach colored carpet and dark purple velvet drapes. For wall coverings he had gold-flecked rice paper and around the room he arranged his oriental art. Circular mirrors became part of the semicircular window arches, and crystal balls were attached to cord pendants which, when pulled, turned on the mirror lights. This apartment came to be known to some as "Taliesin the Third" and to others as "Taliesin East."

It was demolished in 1968.

Frank Lloyd Wright writings & publications

In *The Natural House*, Wright described his Usonian House, the simplified and scaled-down version of his Prairie House. Essentially the Usonian House was intended to be moderately priced, partially prefabricated, and constructed of wood, glass, and brick under a slab roof.

1954 BUILDINGS

E. Clarke Arnold House, Columbus, Wisconsin.

Beth Sholom Synagogue, Elkins Park, Pennsylvania.

Cedric G. Boulter House, Cincinnati, Ohio.

John E. Christian House, Lafayette, Indiana. (*Below, left and right.*)

John J. Dobkins House, Canton, Ohio.

Ellis A. Feiman House, Canton, Ohio.

Louis B. Frederick House, Barrington Hills, Illinois.

Maurice Greenberg House, Dousman, Wisconsin.

Isaac Newton Hagan House, Chalkhill, Pennsylvania.

Willard H. Keland House, Racine, Wisconsin.

Harold Price Jnr. House, Bartlesville, Oklahoma.

Harold Price Snr. House, Paradise Valley, Arizona.

William L. Thaxton House, Bunker Hill, Texas.

Abraham Wilson House, Millstone, New Jersey.

PROJECTS

Barnsdall Park Municipal Gallery, Los Angeles, California.

Christian Science Reading Room, Riverside, Illinois.

Tipshus Clinic, Stockton, California.

Cornwell House, West Goshen, Pennsylvania.

Freund Department Store, San Salvador, El Salvador.

Rebhuhn House, Fort Meyers, Florida.

Schwenn House, Verona, Wisconsin.

Beth Sholom Synagogue

Old York Road at Foxcroft, Elkins Park, Pennsylvania

Guided tours by appointment only.

A hexagon that tends toward an equilateral triangle infuses every element of the design. This plan, according to Wright, mirrored the shape of cupped hands—the cupped hands of God in which the congregation safely rests. The main sanctuary is suspended from a 160-ton steel tripod frame, each beam 117 feet long, so that a full upper floor, the great hall of the synagogue, with 1,030 seats, directly above the sanctuary below, is completely free of any internal supports. The separate Sisterhood Sanctuary, below the great hall, seats 250.

The synagogue is constructed from concrete, steel, aluminum, glass, fiberglass, and oiled walnut. A double layer of translucent panels—2,100 square feet of blasted white

corrugated wire glass outside and 2,000 square feet of reinforced cream white corrugated fiberglass inside, with a five-inch air space—transmits soft light to the interior and provides insulation.

The Arks that hold the Torahs of both sanctuaries incorporate Wrightian design elements and the impressive chandelier that hangs above the congregation reveals Wright returning to Prairie art glass for a traditional statement. The three ridges of the synagogue symbolize the flames of the menorah while the entry canopy geometrically represents the hands of the rabbi joined to pronounce a benediction.

In addition to the sanctuaries, the building contains lounges, offices, and meeting rooms, all of which can be accessed from the main entrance. Typically, Wright also found space for two of his beloved fireplaces.

At night, artificial interior light makes the whole building glow, expressing the idea of the Torah as light, and Mount Sinai as the mount of light—integrating Jewish symbolism with architectural expression. This structure has been designated by the American Institute of Architects as one of the seventeen American buildings designed by Frank Lloyd Wright to be retained as an example of his contribution to American culture.

1955

1955 BUILDINGS

Dallas (Kalita Humphreys) Theater Center.

Randall Fawcett House, Los Banos, California.
(*Right and far right.*)

Max Hoffman House III, Manursing Island,
Rye, New York.

Toufic Kalil House, Manchester, New
Hampshire. (*Opposite, below.*)

Donald Lovness House, Stillwater, Minnesota.

Theodore A. Pappas House, St. Louis,
Missouri.

Plaza Hotel Apartment, Frank Lloyd Wright,
New York City, New York.

John L. Rayward House "Tirranna," New
Canaan, Connecticut.

Robert H. Sunday House, Marshalltown,
Iowa.

Tonkens House, Amberley Village, Ohio.

D. H. Turkel House, Detroit, Michigan.

PROJECTS

Adelman House, Whitefish Bay, Wisconsin.
Barton House, Downer's Grove, Illinois.
Blumberg House, Des Moines, Iowa.
Boswell House I, Cincinnati, Ohio.
Christian Science Church, Bolinas, California.
Coats House, Hillsborough, California.
Cooke House, Virginia Beach, Virginia (Scheme II).
Dlesk House, Manestee, Michigan.
Gillin House, Hollywood, California.
Jankowski House I, Oakland County, Michigan.
Lenkurt Electric Company Administration and
    Manufacturing Building, San Mateo, California.
Miller House, Milford, Michigan.

Morris Guest House, San Francisco, California.
Neuroseum (Hospital and Clinic), Madison,
    Wisconsin.
Oboler House II, Los Angeles, California.
"One Room House," Phoenix, Arizona.
Pieper House, Phoenix, Arizona.
Sussman House, Rye, New York.
Wieland Motel, Hagerstown, Maryland.

*Left and below: Dorothy H. Turkel
House*

Dallas Theater Center

3636 Turtle Creek Boulevard, Dallas, Texas

Terrace above foyer enclosed.
Open for visits when no production is in rehearsal.

The design employs modules with sixty- and 120-degree angles as well as circles. It was the only commissioned theater ever completed from Frank Lloyd Wright's designs. It is a concrete cantilever construction with a 127-ton concrete stage loft built onto the hillside of a one-acre wooded site. The focus of the design is the circular stage drum, extending well above the rest of the concrete mass and containing a forty-foot circular stage, which itself contains a thirty-two-foot turntable. The turntable is divided into thirds, which allows one set to be on stage, one to be struck, and one to be set up for the next scene. The fixed apron, side stages, and two balconies that flank the main stage can provide additional performing space. The complex also includes dressing rooms on three levels and a spiral ramp that leads to the production work-shop areas housed beneath the 466-seat auditorium.

Construction of the theater was about one-quarter complete when Wright died and the Taliesin Associated Architects finished the work.

Donald and Virginia Lovness Residence

10121 83rd North, Stillwater, Minnesota

This single-story, stone and wood structure is one of the last
Usonian Houses and is one of the most innovative of Wright's
designs in the 1950s. It is notable for its elimination of the usual
tunnel gallery without having to add a second floor. Although
the house has only three rooms, discounting bathrooms, it
achieves a high degree of privacy. The master and guest bedrooms form separate wings off the living room. A fireplace is
centered on the back wall and deck-high cabinets at the rear,
near the master bedroom, separate the workspace. Fir mullions
with full and half-bay plate glass articulate the facade. An interesting feature is the three accordion doors, one by Wright and
the other two by Taliesin Fellows.

In 1976, the Lovnesses also built a square plan "one-room
cottage" from plans drawn up by Wright in 1958 and comple-
mented it with furniture
constructed from the first
designs for the Barnsdall
"Hollyhock" house of 1917.
Extra chairs from the cottage
are now in museum collections.

*Left and right:The Lovnesses con-
structed their home and made all
the custom-designed furniture.*

Above, left, and right: Sculptures adorn the exterior and interior of the Lovness House.

1956

In 1956, three years before his death, Wright visited Wales for the first and last time to receive an honorary degree from the University of Wales.

Building work on the Guggenheim finally began in summer of 1956 and it opened to the public on October 21, 1959, six months after Wright died.

Frank Lloyd Wright writings & publications
The Story of the Tower: The Tree That Escaped The Crowded Forest, published by Horizon Press, 1956.

1956 BUILDINGS

Annunciation Greek
   Orthodox Church,
   Wauwatosa, Wisconsin.

Frank Bott House, Kansas
   City, Missouri.

Allan Friedman House,
   Bannockburn, Illinois.

Solomon R. Guggenheim
   Museum, New York City,
   New York.

Hoffman Auto Showroom,
   New York, New York. (*Far
   left.*)

Kundert Clinic, San Louis
   Obispo, California. (*Left.*)

Meyers Clinic, Dayton, Ohio.

Riverview Terrace
   Restaurant, Spring Green,
   Wisconsin.

Dudley Spencer House,
   Wilmington, Delaware.

Eugene VanTamelen House,
   Madison, Wisconsin.

Left: Kundert Clinic

PROJECTS

Boebel House, Boscobel, Wisconsin.

Bramlett Hotel, Memphis, Tennessee.

Golden Beacon skyscraper, Chicago, Illinois.

Gross House, Hackensack, New Jersey.

Hunt House, Scottsdale, Arizona.

Tonkens Loan Office, Cincinnati.

Mile High skyscraper, Chicago, Illinois.

Morris House ("Quietwater"), Stinson Beach, California.

Sports Pavilion, Belmont, Long Island, New York.

O'Keefe House, Santa Barbara, California.

Roberts House, Seattle, Washington.

Schuck House, South Hadley, Massachusetts.

Stillman House, Cornwall on Hudson, New York.

Vallarino Houses, Panama City, Panama.

Solomon R. Guggenheim Museum

Fifth Avenue, New York City (completed 1959)

Semi-restored structure opened to the public, June 28, 1992.

In 1937 the Solomon R. Guggenheim Foundation was formed and Wright was commissioned to provide a building to house their art collection—the Museum of Non-Objective Painting. Wright's original concept, dated 1943, is labeled "ziggurat," and this is still evident in the final plan, the main gallery of which is a quarter-mile long, concrete, cantilevered spiraling ramp, which curves continuously as it rises through seventy-five feet to the glass-domed skylight of the roof. In this spiral building Wright used concrete in inventive structural systems and in bold geometric forms planned on a dominant geometric principle. To Wright the spiral was symbolic of the "organic process." More than the triangle, hexagon, or circle that had been the module for so many of his earlier works, for Wright the spiral was the most exciting form because it existed in three dimensions and because an expanding spiral seemed to defy gravity. Wright expected this sloping structure to counteract the usual dominance of right-angled architecture over the flat plane of a painting.

Wright was engaged in a battle, primarily with New York Commissioner Robert Moses, for sixteen years to build the museum. Over such a long period of time, the costs naturally escalated and, accordingly, the plans were revised time and time again. When he received the notice of construction approval, Wright announced to those in the Taliesin drafting room, "I've been designing this

building for others for twenty-five years; now I'm going to design it for myself." He incorporated all the building commissioners' requirements while altering the angle of the exterior walls of the main gallery several times until he was satisfied that the sky-lighting would provide proper lighting for the paintings. Outside, the cast concrete form is purely sculptural, without any surface decorations, the streamlined exterior setting the pattern for walls and spaces inside. In 1952, the name of the building was changed from the Museum of Non-Objective Painting to the Solomon R. Guggenheim Museum, but Wright apparently took little notice of this in his design, which remained consistent with the original concept.

Building work on the Guggenheim finally began in the summer of 1956, and it opened to the public on October 21, 1959— six months after Wright died. The museum is a late reminder of the architect's creative originality and effortless ability to shock. The museum has been designated by the American Institute of Architects as one of the seventeen American buildings designed by Frank Lloyd Wright to be retained as an example of his architectural contribution to American culture.

Annunciation Greek Orthodox Church

9400 West Congress Street, Wauwatosa, Wisconsin

Open to visitors.

This masterpiece of form and structure is hardly recognizable by traditional Greek Orthodox standards yet leaves no doubts about its religious purpose. The main level plan forms a Greek cross that infuses most elements of detail. The structure and roof form of this church is a concrete shell, originally surfaced with a blue ceramic mosaic tile later replaced by a synthetic plastic resin, supported on thousands of ball bearings. The truss is held by four concrete piers at the ends of the inward curving walls of the Greek cross. Inside, the sanctuary has no interior supports to obstruct the view of the worshippers and no parishioner sits more than sixty feet from the sacristy. Circular stairs lead to an upper level which seats a further 560 congregants. The balcony, with its disc-like shape, has outer edges that are gravity-supported by the circular truss that it helps to stabilize laterally, and further unifies the composition.

Light enters the building through semicircular windows and 325 transparent glass spheres that separate the edge of the upper wall and the domed roof. Wright did not live to see the completed building.

1957

Frank Lloyd Wright writings & publications

A Testament, published by Horizon Press, 1957.
In this work Wright stated that his only influences were the
"Lieber Master" (Louis Sullivan), Dankmar Adler, John
Roebling (the architect of the Brooklyn Bridge in New York),
Walt Whitman, and Ralph Waldo Emerson. He wrote: "My
work is original not only in fact but in spiritual fiber," although
he did state that in the architecture of the Mayans and the
Japanese he found, not inspiration, but confirmation of many of
his ideas about organic architecture.

Right: Walter Rudin House.

1957 BUILDINGS

William P. Boswell House II, Indian Hill, Ohio.

Erdman Prefab Houses, Upper Great Lakes:
La Fond, St Joseph, Minnesota.
James McBean, Rochester, Minnesota.
Joseph Mollica, Bayside, Wisconsin.
Walter Rudin, Madison, Wisconsin.

Erdman Prefab Houses, Metro, Chicago:
Carl Post House, Barrington Hills, Illinois.
Don Duncan House, Lisle, Illinois. (1957)
Frank Iber, Plover, Wisconsin.
Arnold Jackson, Madison, Wisconsin.

Erdman Prefab houses, East:
William Cass House,
Richmond, New York.
Socrates Zaferiou, Blauvelt,
New York.

**Fasbender Medical Clinic,
Hastings, Minnesota.**
(*Opposite, below.*)

Conrad E. Gordon House,
Aurora, Oregon.

**Juvenile Cultural Study
Center Building A, University
of Wichita, Kansas.**

Sterling Kinney House,
Amarillo, Texas.

**Lindholm Service Station,
Cloquet, Minnesota.**

Right: Carl Post House.

Opposite, above: Duncan House

*Opposite, below: Fasbender
Medical Clinic.*

PHILLIPS

PHILLIPS 66

WORLD'S ONLY
FRANK LLOYD WRIGHT
service station

Marin County Civic Center, San Raphael, California (construction through 1966): Post Office, San Raphael, California.

Arthur Miller and Marilyn Monroe House.

Carl Schulz House, St. Joseph, Michigan. (*Opposite: above and below.*)

Paul J. Trier House, Des Moines, Iowa.

Robert G. Walton House, Modesto, California.

Duey Wright House, Wausau, Wisconsin.

Wyoming Valley Grammar School, Spring Green, Wisconsin.

Left: Lindholm Service Station

PROJECTS

Adams House, St. Paul, Minnesota.

Nezam Ameri Palace, Tehran, Iran.

Arizona State Capitol, Papago Park, Phoenix, Arizona.

Baghdad Cultural Center, Baghdad, Iraq.

University of Baghdad, Baghdad, Iraq.

Bimson House, Phoenix, Arizona.

Brooks House, Middleton, Wisconsin.

Hartman House, Lansing, Michigan.

Hennesy Houses (two projects), Smoke Rise, New Jersey.

Herberger House, Maricopa County, Arizona.

Highway Motel, Madison, Wisconsin.

Fisher Housing Project, Whiteville, North Carolina.

Hoyer House, Maricopa County, Arizona.

Juvenile Study Center Building B, University of Wichita, Kansas.

Gate Lodge for Fallingwater, Bear Run, Pennsylvania.

McKinney House, Cloquet, Minnesota.

Miller House, near Roxbury, Connecticut.

Mills House II, Princeton, New Jersey.

U.S. Rubber Company Model Exhibition Houses (exhibition project), New York.

Moreland House, Austin, Texas.

Postal Telegraph Building, Baghdad, Iraq.

Post Office, Spring Green, Wisconsin.

Schanbacher Store, Springfield, Illinois.

Shelton House, Long Island, New York.

Sottil House, Cuernavaca, Mexico.

Stracke House, Appleton, Wisconsin.

Wedding Chapel for the Claremont Hotel, Berkeley, California.

Wilson House, Morgantown, North Carolina.

Zieger House, Grosse Isalnd, Michigan.

Left and below: Walton House

Marin County Civic Center

North San Pedro Road at U.S. 101, San Raphael, California

Post Office
Administration Building
Hall of Justice
Juvenile Cultural Study Center
Open to the public during regular university session hours.

The Civic Center includes a main Administration Building and contiguous Hall of Justice of similar concrete coated with polymer paint. Built out of pre-cast and pre-stressed concrete and steel, the construction technique for these buildings made use of segmentation and expansion joints so that they would withstand significant seismic shocks, as the region lies on the famous San Andreas Fault.

Wright's sole works for the U.S. Government, the Post Office, is a nearly circular structure of concrete block and forms. It sits across the street, at the foot of the hill below the

Administration Building. The first, compact, plan had to be enlarged in the mail-sorting area, disrupting the original proportions.

The wings that comprise the Marin County Administration Building and the Hall of Justice reach out from behind the domed library center, behind the commanding pylon (a ventilation tower intended by Wright to serve also as a radio antenna). In Wright's master plan for the site, a 584-foot Administration Building and an 880-foot long Hall of Justice would bridge the valleys between three adjacent hills on the site. Each of the two wings seeks a distant hill complementing the spaces between them. The focal point of the plan was a dome, 80 feet in diameter and crowned by a 172-foot golden tower. Modifications to Wright's original design, to suit the client, were largely in the area of adjusting sizes of certain rooms within the Hall of Justice (which features moveable walls) to their specific uses and integrating these with a multi-level arcaded format. Originally the central atriums were to be open to the sky but practical

Above and left: The focal point and center of the Marin County Civic Center is a flattened dome and a gold tower.

considerations led to this scheme being replaced by barrel-vaulted skylights.

Two buildings were originally planned for the Juvenile Cultural Study Center, a classroom and office building, and an elementary laboratory school. The classroom and office were built but the elementary school, which might have been the more interesting of the two in its use of concentric circular segments as unit modules, was never built. Cast concrete, metals, and expanses of glass constitute the rectangular units on either side of the patio of the Study Center. Each wing is two stories high, with classrooms and office space, and courtyards symmetrically placed about the patio axis, all on an eight-foot-square unit module.

The pylon, which was intended to be a radio tower, was the dramatic exclamation point in the design of the futuristic development. The project for Marin County was the nearest Wright got to realizing his dream of a utopian city. The design and construction of this complex was underway when Wright died in 1959 and it was finished under the aegis of Aaron Green, William Wesley Peters, and the Taliesin Associated Architects. It gives us a vision of what Wright's dream city— Broadacre City—could have been, and also exemplifies how innovative and forward looking Wright's architectural designs were, even into his nineties.

Below and right: The barrel-vaulted skylights and the decorative grillwork of the interior.

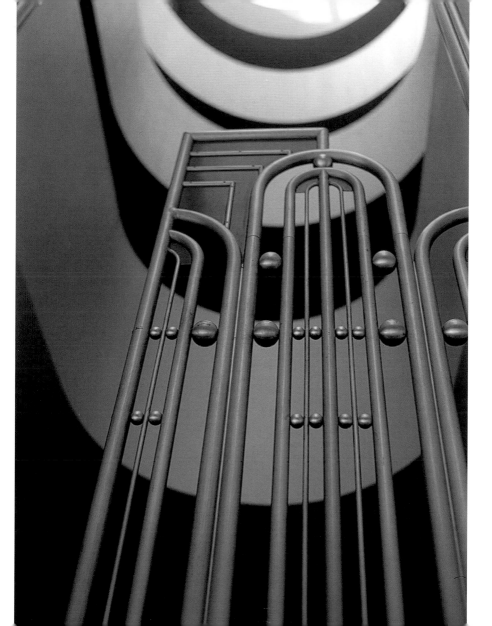

1958

Frank Lloyd Wright writings & publications
The Living City, published by Horizon Press, 1958.

1958 BUILDINGS

George Ablin House, Bakersfield, California.

Lockridge, McIntyre and Whalen Clinic, Whitefish, Montana.

Joseph Mollica House, Bayside, Wisconsin.

Paul Olfelt House, St. Louis Park, Minnesota.

Seth Petersen Cottage, Lake Delton, Wisconsin. (*Right.*)

Pilgrim Congregational Church, Redding, California (partly built). (*Overleaf*)

Donald Stromquist House, Bountiful, Utah.

PROJECTS

Dr. George and Millie Ablin Residence

4260 Country Club Drive, Bakersfield, California

The Ablin House, with its outside L-plan (240 degrees on an equilateral parallelogram grid), based on a triangular module, is sited on a knoll next to the Bakersfield Country Club. In this house there is a striking contrast between the large south facing living room of glass and wood and the pool-side main construction of salmon concrete block—some are perforated to provide windows.

The master bedrooms and a study are in one wing, while the children's rooms, with several bathrooms, are in the other. The two are joined together by the large workspace with its pierced light-admitting block, glazed with plexiglass, and the enormous living room. Leading to the central core of entry room, living room, dining room, and high-ceilinged kitchen is a covered walkway.

Below and right: The living room interior and exterior.

Cedar shingles, the copper roofing originally requested was too expensive, and Philippine mahogany are also principal construction materials. The low pitched, wood-shingled gable roofs extend outward to provide shade for the glass walls, terraces, and the entry walk.

Masonry walls are battered and vertical mortar joints were filled to the surface, horizontals deeply raked to emphasize horizontality. The mason, however, rubbed all surface-level joints smooth thus leaving a visible line between textured block which necessitated painting the masonry to make the whole surface smooth.

The house contains many fine examples of Wright's free-standing wood furniture, including geometric wooden "light-tower" lamps.

Left: Concrete block is perforated to provide light.

Above: The house contains examples of furniture designed by Wright.

1959

Wright returned to Taliesin West in 1959 after the stressful Guggenheim Museum project that had taken its toll on his health. Now aged 91 Wright was operated on in Phoenix to remove an intestinal obstruction, but despite his frailty he appeared to come through the operation successfully. Five days later, on April 9, 1959, Wright died. His body was taken back to his old home in Spring Green, Wisconsin, where it was placed in the family burial ground a few hundred yards from Taliesin, next to his mother and Mamah Cheney. There he remained for twenty-six years, until 1985 when Olgivanna died; her last wish was that in death they should be together, so his remains were disinterred and taken to Taliesin West in Arizona, where their ashes were mingled together and buried in a new grave.

Frank Lloyd Wright writings & publications
Drawings for a Living Architecture, published by Horizon Press, 1959.

1959 BUILDINGS

William Cass House, Richmond, New York.

Grady Gammage Memorial Auditorium, Arizona State University, Tempe, Arizona (*Left*).

PROJECTS

Art Gallery, Arizona State University, Tempe, Arizona.

Donohoe House, Phoenix, Arizona.

Furgatch House, San Diego, California.

Mann House, Putnam County, New York.

Penfield House II, Willoughby, Ohio.

Daniel Wieland House, Hagerstown, Maryland.

Gilbert Wieland House, Hagerstown, Maryland.

Grady Gammage Memorial Auditorium

Arizona State University, Apache Boulevard at Mill Avenue, Tempe, Arizona

Stage workshop loading ramp raised to ground level.
Half-hour tours are conducted on Saturday afternoons
    only.

Wright's last non-residential design to be built was the
Gammage Memorial Auditorium of the Arizona State University
that seats 3,000 persons in the continental style—it has wide
spacing between the rows and no center aisle. This public space
was designed as a center for performing arts with a concert hall,
theater, teaching spaces, and offices. The plan of the auditorium
building is actually composed of two circles of unequal size: the
larger circle contains the promenades, lobbies, and audience
hall while the smaller circle houses the dressing rooms, work-
shops, teaching areas, offices, and the auditorium stage. The

*Below and right: The theme of
the circular motif from the exterior
is continued in the interior
decoration.*

140-foot wide stage features a steel acoustic shell that can be mechanically adjusted to accommodate the sounds of a full orchestra and accompanying choir stage, or collapsed and stored against the rear wall during theatrical presentations. The auditorium has three levels: floor, grand tier, and balcony. The grand tier is suspended forward of the rear auditorium wall on a 145-foot-long steel beam, providing the space underneath with the same reverberation characteristics as uncovered spaces.

Left and below: An arcade of 50 columns wraps around the facade and supports the concrete shell roof of the Grady Gammage Memorial Auditorium.

The building has a circular arcade of fifty tall concrete columns, cast on the site, each rising fifty-five feet to support the outer roof. The deck of the roof is gypsum and shell-thin concrete while the exterior walls are made of brick and a marble like composition called marblecrete in a desert-rose finish.

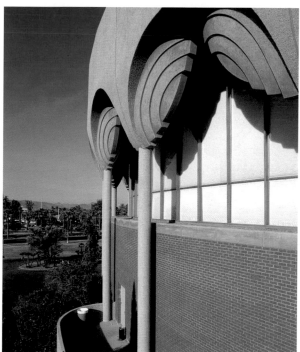

Interior brick and sand-finish plaster with acoustical tile, walnut trim, and reinforced-concrete floors complete the list of major construction materials.

The circular motif of the construction is repeated in the decorative lights of the 200-foot long pedestrian walkways and bridge that take the audience from the sunken lawns and parking lot to the auditorium where "No Smoking" is a design feature. No ashtrays were provided in either auditorium or lobby.

Dr. Edward La Fond House

29710 Kipper Road, St Joseph, Minnesota

Dr La Fond learned about Wright's designs and commissioned the house through Erdman's company. It is one of the last of the Erdman Prefabs. La Fond was visiting the Erdman offices concerning a building for his medical practice when he saw plans for the Prefab #1 lying on a table. Erdman tried to persuade his client to build one of his prefabs but the doctor persisted with his demand for the Wright design.

The building is constructed with standard concrete block. It has three bedrooms on the first floor and a full basement under the entire main floor to accommodate four additional bedrooms. Natural light is admitted through window wells in the ground and the house is rotated seventeen degrees east of south to take advantage of the morning sun and to bring the sun to the rear wall during the long summer days.

The client never contacted Taliesin and employed his brother as the carpenter for the project. Original asphalt shingles with horizontal ribbing have been replaced with "timberline" random asphalt and a wood deck added between terrace and kitchen. The house is in perfect original condition except for a sliding glass door designed and approved recently by the Taliesin Associated Architects.

First Christian Church

6750 North 7th Avenue, Phoenix, Arizona

Guided tours by appointment.

Designed by Wright and built after his death, this was the last project to be completed in Arizona. Wright first produced plans of a university campus for the Southwest Christian Seminary in 1951. When the university failed to proceed, the First Christian Church decided to go ahead with the chapel, starting work on it in 1971, twelve years after Wright's death. The building is supported by twenty-three triangular steel and concrete pillars while a narrower range of columns, which frame the clerestory windows, are crowned by a pyramidal roof and seventy-seven-foot spire.

Light that filters through colored glass insets in the spire falls onto the floor of the diamond-shaped sanctuary. The church features a stained-glass window by a member of the Taliesin Fellowship, as well as a 120-foot, freestanding bell tower with four unequal sides that has the appearance of being triangular.

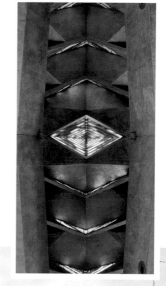

Left and right: Triangular steel and concrete pillars support the First Christian Church building.

Above and overleaf: Colored glass insets let light filter through to the floor of the sanctuary.

From a distance it seems that Wright spent much of his life embroiled in controversy. From the quarrels within his own family, and between his parents, the emotional conflicts he brought upon himself by abandoning his first wife, and mother of his six children, for another married woman, his noisy pacifism during World War II, which brought him many new enemies—not to mention his anti-establishment stance toward fellow architects, other people's architecture, planning regulations as well as bureaucracy and society in general. Always arrogant, obdurate, and able to make enemies with ease, he also made strong friendships and inspired tremendous loyalty from his followers. Throughout his career architects who were more conventional than Wright opposed his unorthodox methods. Wright's view of architecture was essentially romantic although he often paid lip service to the rational systems called for by mass-produced building but his efforts in those directions seemed halfhearted at best.

By the time of his death, Frank Lloyd Wright was recognized as the greatest architect that America had produced to date. He designed his buildings to be lived in, and experienced in person—not to be seen in drawings and photographs. He left a rich heritage of completed buildings of almost uniform splendor but few of his adherents could match the special genius reflected in his works. He was essentially an idiosyncratic architect whose influence was immense but whose pupils were few.

The Taliesin Associated Architects (TAA) is still building Wright's designs today.

Index